COUNTRY TALES

OLD GILLIES

ooooo

Tom Quinn

DAVID & CHARLES

Cover photographs supplied by the author

The material in this book was originally published in a fuller form under the
title *Tales from the Water's Edge* (David & Charles, 1991)

A DAVID & CHARLES BOOK

First published in the UK in 1998

A catalogue record for this book is available from the British Library.

ISBN 0 7153 0834 3

Printed in the UK by Mackays of Chatham plc
for David & Charles
Brunel House   Newton Abbot   Devon

CONTENTS

———— ◦◦◦◦◦ ————

AUTHOR'S NOTE

———— ooooo ————

When this book was first published nearly ten years ago, the gillies and riverkeepers whose stories it contains were either nearing or had reached the end of their careers. All have now retired; some, sadly, have died. Their careers had started decades earlier, at a time when our rivers were still relatively unpolluted; when salmon and trout were still plentiful and when the fishermen for whom they worked were part of an upper class, leisured set which has now all but vanished.

But even by the 1980s, when I travelled round the country to meet the men whose lives are recounted here, they were working with the newly rich and with people from a far wider range of social and economic backgrounds than ever before. Part of the appeal of the sport for the new generation of fishermen was the company of their gillies, without whom much of the pleasure of fishing would disappear.

I suspect that gillies have always been seen as a race apart. Even in the days when servants were treated as though they were invisible, the gillie knew so much more about the river and worked so closely with his charges that it must have been difficult, if not impossible, to remain aloof. There is also the undeniable fact that gillies tend to a remarkably high degree to be excellent company, fine storytellers, convivial and even charismatic. The ultimate example is, of course, Queen Victoria's gillie, John Brown, whose close relationship with the Queen has been the subject of a recent highly successful film, and whose career is discussed in more detail in the main introduction to this book.

Most people probably have a rough idea what a gillie does, but the details of the job, the precise nature of the day to day work involved, will be something of a mystery, unless one is lucky enough to have met and got to know one of these remarkable characters. Like the gamekeeper, the gillie avoids the limelight. He helps with a sport that rarely if ever appears on television or in the newspapers, and he usually works alone, or with a few regular clients, in a remote part of the country. Entry to his world is, as it were, by invitation only. But if it does nothing else I hope this revised and updated book will extend that invitation to a much wider public.

INTRODUCTION

———— ∞∞∞ ————

The word gillie comes from the Gaelic word for a sports-man's or a Highland chief's attendant, but it is an unfor-tunate word in that it gives many people the impression that the kind of work the gillie does is unique to Scotland. This is far from the truth; there are riverkeepers who perform the role of gillie as far south as Devon and Sussex; there are gillies in Wales and Cumbria and there are gillying riverkeepers in East Yorkshire and in Wiltshire and Hampshire.

In Scotland the word gillie still applies to an individual who helps with the fishing and, when necessary, with the stalking and grouse shooting, so there is no reason why it should not apply to many of those riverkeepers south of the Border who help guide and tutor both the novice and the more experienced fisherman.

Many gillies and riverkeepers spend their lives on one or two short stretches of the same river. Some riverkeeping families – most notably the Lunns of Hampshire – have worked for gener-ations on the same water. Most find the life so compelling that they will suffer low wages and poor prospects rather than seek a change. The gillie is not a man out to make money or to enjoy an easy life. Gillying and riverkeeping are hard work; work that can mean dangerous encounters with poachers as well as the perpetual battle against pollution. Gillying and riverkeeping are full-time jobs; full time in the sense that, day or night, winter or summer, the needs of the river and its fish come first.

In many ways Queen Victoria helped create the image of the

loyal but proud Highland servant or gillie through her close relationship with John Brown. Although a servant, Brown was treated with enormous respect and affection by the Queen. So much so that she insisted - to the scandalised outrage of some people – that on her death his photograph should be buried with her.

Queen Victoria was the first modern monarch to make a habit of going regularly to the wilds of Scotland. She helped revive the interest in tartans, Highland games, stalking and salmon fishing. Soon the aristocracy began to follow and going to Scotland to stalk red deer and to fish for salmon became, and have remained, fashionable things to do. But without a gillie, fishing and stalking were inconceivable.

All the gillies and riverkeepers who agreed to be interviewed for this book said that they would not have chosen any other career. Some had tried other work, but could not settle to it. None was living in circumstances that could be described as more than comfortable and all had lived what most of us would consider a hard life in terms of hours worked and holidays taken. All the gillies I met and talked to had the dour good humour that seems such a hallmark of their calling. All were patient and helpful and some were able to show me the rivers where they worked.

The stories of their lives are, in part at least, stories of great change. Most obviously fishing tackle has developed out of all recognition during the past fifty or sixty years, from the days of great brass reels and heavy greenheart rods to the ultra-light carbon and boron rods of the 1990s. But there have also been enormous changes in the kinds of people the gillies and riverkeepers now take out on the river. Some of the old aristocrats still survive and they have grown old with their gillies, but there is new blood now and many foreign anglers come to fish the great trout and salmon rivers of England, Scotland and Wales.

Transport has changed, too. A horse and trap would at one time meet the visiting angler and take him from the railway station to the lodge or hotel where he might stay for several weeks. These days anglers may arrive by helicopter. The speed of modern communications can mean that the fisherman or woman is whisked up to the Spey for just a day or two before he heads off back to New York, Geneva or London. But at the still point of this world remain the gillies and riverkeepers and the stories they tell of their lives and adventures are the subject of this book.

I have talked to gillies and riverkeepers from many different parts of the country. Some think of themselves as riverkeepers and not gillies, but they all have a devotion to their rivers that unites them in a fascinating brotherhood. This book is an attempt, however partial and limited, to give some account of that brotherhood. *Country Tales: Old Gillies* is also an attempt to record the memories of some of our oldest riverkeepers – men like Joe Taylor, who worked for more than sixty years on the same river – before they fade forever into history.

The "Bethune" Line Winder.

(HARDY'S PATENT)

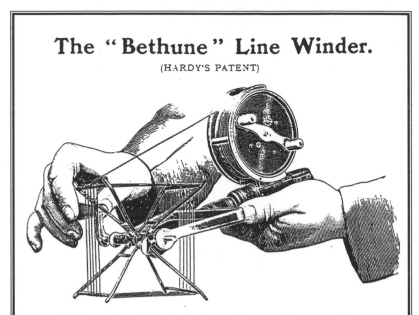

THE invention of C. C. Bethune, Esq., and is one of the best and most compact yet invented. The illustration shows it in use. The reel is put on the handle, exactly as on a rod butt, the fittings being the same. The winder works between two spiral springs, and can be oscillated in winding, thus the line is not all wound in one place, but is evenly distributed.

In winding line off the reel, the small thumb screw should be eased. When as much line as desired has been wound off, this screw is then tightened, and keeps all taut. When the line is being wound back on to the reel again, the thumb screw should be eased a little to allow winder to travel steadily.

When line is wound off reel on to winder, both the reel and winder may be hung up until they are again wanted.

They are made in two sizes, Trout and Salmon, and packed in neat cedar wood boxes, with slide lids.

To Pack.—Simply unscrew arms and handle.

☞ FOR LANDING NETS, SEE PAGES 285 TO 296.

SIXTY YEARS A GILLIE

———— ooooo ————

Joe Taylor was a gillie and riverkeeper on the River Eden in Cumbria for over sixty years. He started work on the Low House Estate straight from school at the age of fourteen and stayed till the day he died at the age of seventy-seven in 1992. At the start of his career he did general keepering work on the estate before taking on the job of full-time gillie in the thirties.

Joe probably held the record for the greatest number of years spent working as a gillie for one employer on one stretch of river. And in a remarkable double he also held the record, at 41lb, for the heaviest salmon ever caught on rod and line from the Eden. Surely the ultimate tribute to the skills of the professional gillie?

But Joe always insisted that he couldn't be sure his fish was the record. 'I wouldn't like to say because I knew a fish of 44½lb was once taken in the nets at Armathwaite Castle and anyway a fish is just a fish, however big it is. You've not to be proud to have caught the biggest because it doesn't matter really.'

Joe was a remarkably animated and sprightly character even during his final illnesss. Long after he officially retired he continued to spend as much of his time as he could on the river, both to fish and to take out clients who had been with him for many years. He never thought about giving it all up. 'Well, the thing about gillying on a river is that you make friends with so many people. In fact, I would say that my strongest memories of all my years on the Eden are memories of good companionship. Yes, all the people who fished here absolutely doted on me!'

Joe roared with laughter, but despite the jokes or perhaps

because of them, he was clearly a very popular figure. On the day I visited him he had just returned from lunch with a client who had come all the way from South Africa just to see him. And for years another client insisted on being accompanied by Joe even when he was fishing miles away on Tweed.

The Low House Estate, roughly 3,000 acres of hilly well-wooded country, was owned by the Ecroyds, who were mill-owners before the great depression of the thirties. Joe worked for the head of two generations of the family:

'When I started at Low House I worked for old Mr William Ecroyd. He's been dead for many years. At the end I worked for young Mr Peter. When the mill business slumped the family sold up, but in a way they were too quick to sell because if they'd held on a bit they might have done much better. There was a boom in demand for bandages when the war came and the mills that remained did very well. But, of course, the Ecroyd family had already sold up by then.

'In my early days the fishing was totally different from what it is now. There was nothing commercial about it at all. All the fishing was just given to Mr Ecroyd's friends. Mind you the gillie's work was still hard. When I started I was hauling four boats. There were twenty-two male servants up at the house in the twenties. Now there's just one – my grandson.'

Joe clearly enjoyed the family association with Low House and indeed with the keepering profession:

'Five generations of my family had been involved with this type of work. My grandfather was a headkeeper up at Bassenthwaite Lake and my father was underkeeper at Castletown before he came here in 1924 to be headkeeper. Then my son worked for a time here at Low House – he's now working for the Duke of Sutherland – and my grandson works here looking after the fishing in the early part of the year.

'I think the real difference between fishing in the twenties and thirties and now is that then it was just seen as a bit of fun. I'll give you an example of the difference in attitude. Old Mr Edward used to say to me when he wanted to fish, "I'll see you at ten tomorrow morning Joe." So I'd get everything ready for him the next day. He'd then turn up in the morning and as like as not he'd sniff the air and say, "It's not a good day Joe, I think we'll give it a rest." And that would be that. No fishing for the rest of the day. No one would ever do that these days. There's too much money involved.

'The whole thing became much more commercial when Edward Ecroyd died. I think it was in 1952 and the death duties were so great that the fishing had to start paying its way. In fact everyone on the estate was expected to try to make a contribution to the estate to try to keep it together. My job at that time was to fish the river commercially with rod and line. I had 110 fish in that first year to my own rod. All my fish were sold – including my forty-one pounder. There were a lot of big fish around then and I landed quite a few that year over 30lb.

'I always enjoyed my fishing. I'd started with the trout as a small boy so I was already fishing by the time I started here in 1929. At that time there was a lot of netting on the river. It didn't really produce much money – and not many fish either – because with no deep freezes all you could do with the fish was give them to local people round about.'

Joe was a mine of tales of massive fish played and landed, as well as played and lost, but he was always asked about the battle with his own forty-one pounder:

'Yes, that big one certainly gave us a bit of sport. Mind you I knew it was something really beefy as soon as it struck. After I hooked it I remember it went off upstream and took virtually all my line in spite of the fact that I was giving it as much stick as I dared. Anyway, I was in the boat and just as I was about to lift the anchor to follow the fish up the river, it turned. As it came back past the boat I could see it and I remember thinking, Christ it's a thirty. Just at that moment it saw me and headed for the sea. This time I really did have to up anchor and away – not an easy matter when you think I was fishing in 30ft of water. After that I lost contact with the fish for a while. I thought I might even have lost him, but then suddenly I was back in touch and I played him for a while in deep water before he came to the top between the boat and the bank.

'I was terrified he'd go back into the deep water, but as he passed the boat the next time I managed to net him. I must admit I was very lucky because that fish wasn't really beaten at all by that stage. And I still didn't realise how big he was. Apart from anything else I'd never seen one that big before.

'By this time my wife had rowed the bailiff across to see the fish. He looked at it and said, "Hell that's more than thirty". He thought it was about 38lb. It was dark by this time and when we'd gone back over the river to the house my wife said she'd carry the fish in – she was a damned good 'un – but as soon as she grabbed its tail she announced "I can't carry that," so I knew it had to be big.

'In the end I got pretty fed up with that fish because so many people came to see it. I couldn't get away from them.'

If he was lucky that time Joe also had his fair share of bad luck and near misses, as he explained.

'I can remember one bad day in particular. I was gillying for a Mr Crispin and we caught a fish of about 15lb. We caught it first time down the pool so Mr Crispin thought we were going to have a red-letter day. After we landed it he was so pleased he tied a bit of old rag round the wrist of the fish's tail so it could be held up for a photograph. And we had to go and get Mrs Crispin for the photograph. She took his picture with it and then he took hers with it. We had a right carry-on.

'At the end of the day I put Mr Crispin across the river so he could go to his hotel and I rowed back home. It was dark by this time, but I'd noticed the fish was dirty so before I went to put it away I thought I'd give it a quick wash. I started washing it in the river holding it by the piece of rag round its tail when all of a sudden it slipped away from me into about 12ft of water.

'Well, my heart stopped. All I could think about was the fact that Mr Crispin had been so proud of that fish. And it wasn't as if we'd gone on to have a great day. We hadn't caught another fish. I had visions of that fish floating off down the river so I called Lizzie, my wife, and we got a flashlight and rowed back out on to the river and it was pitch dark by this time. She took the oars and I put the torch under the water to look for the fish. We went away down the river and not a sight of it. Again and again we tried, up and down the river through the darkness and then, by some miracle, I spotted it. We dropped the anchor and let the boat carefully down the river to where I thought I'd seen it. We found it again, just a pale shape down in the depths of the water. We tried the net, but the water was just too deep. Luckily I had the salmon fly rod in the boat, so I wound the fly up to the top eye and put the rod down deep into the water. I don't know how I did it but I hooked the fish again and Lizzie netted it. Boy, I can't tell you how pleased I was to get that fish back – Mr Crispin would have murdered me if I hadn't.

'I was very lucky to get that fish, but I've been pretty lucky with a number of other fish. I remember once fishing with an old Hardy multiplier. It was a nice reel, but it was a bugger for getting overruns and sure enough on this day – I was spinning at the time – I cast out my prawn and the line immediately went into a bird's nest. It wasn't a really bad one and I was just in the process of untangling it when a good fish hit the prawn. I shoved the rod between my legs and immediately pulled up the anchor. Meanwhile I watched the top of the rod and played the fish by moving the boat up and down the river. At the same time I carried on trying to untangle the mess around the reel.

'I had my fly rod in the boat so I thought if I can make a loop in the end of the fly line, cut the spinning line above the bird's nest and then tie it to the loop, I might still land the fish.

'So that's what I did. And I got away with it. I played that fish on the fly rod and landed it. Mind you if it had jumped just once early on that would have been the end of it. I wouldn't have had an earthly.'

By the early 1990s most of Joe's clients had been coming to fish with him for twenty or thirty years and the fishing was mostly taken by a small syndicate. There were four miles of water to cover, but in this remote part of Cumbria, about ten miles north of Penrith, near the village of Armathwaite, there were few problems with poachers.

'There wasn't much poaching here at all, but that's just as well when you think that there were only about six bailiffs for 40 miles of water on the Eden. I knew, too, that the poaching situation was much worse on, say, the Border Esk. Our big problem wasn't poaching, it was pollution. I think it was all the insecticides and pesticides washing into the river that caused the terrible UDN [Ulcerative Dermal Necrosis].

'I remember in the mid-sixties when the farmers started to use chemicals in a big way and we had terrible UDN I used to go out at nights with my son and we gaffed out nearly eighty really big diseased fish in just ten days. That included a hell of a lot of thirty-pounders. We never had the disease before then.'

Joe's troubles were always confined to the eternal problem of putting fish on the bank. His clients, he always insisted, were never difficult.

'Most people know that they are better off if they take your advice and, in fact, in all my years I only had one chap who thought he'd do it his own way. I remember I met him at the Red Lion in Armathwaite and while I talked to him there I thought, my, he knows his onions, the way he's talking.

'Anyway, the next morning I fixed up his tackle and told him what to do. We got nicely started in the boat and saw one or two fish moving. He hadn't had a fish, so after a while he said "I'm fishing too heavy". I told him that if he felt he was using too much weight he should do what he thought best. He fished lighter and the next minute another angler fishing nearby – using heavy tackle that I'd set up – caught a fish. My man didn't say anything, but when the other angler caught another fish my man said "You know, I think I'll change my weight". He went back to the tackle I'd set up for him and eventually caught a fish.'

Flies and spinners were used on the Eden, but as Joe explained, the days of the winged fly seemed to be over. 'Yes, it was mostly tube flies by the time we'd reached the 1980s and 1990s and spinners, and it has to be said that for every fish you get on a fly in the early part of the year you'll get three on a spinner. We used to spin using Devon minnows but the Eden is really a spring river. It opens on 15 January and closes on 14 October.'

Only once in his long career was Joe tempted to leave Low House. He was asked to go and work for a client who was also a great friend. After the initial offer Joe heard nothing so he mentioned it to his friend a while later. His friend explained that he'd gone to Joe's boss, Peter Ecroyd, and explained that he wanted to offer Joe a job away from the estate. Joe's boss had said, 'You'll get Joe over my dead body' and the client had left it at that.

Joe always found the idea of being fought over highly amusing: 'He was a great friend of mine and he'd have been a great man to work for, but I'd been so long with the Ecroyds by then that I doubt if I could have settled to another life, so perhaps it's just as well that nothing came of it.'

AN ANGLER IN THE WATERMEADOWS

◦◦◦◦◦

David Morris was born in Houghton, Hampshire, in the valley of the most famous trout river in the world: the Test. He spent almost the whole of his working life on the river and worked with some of the best-known riverkeepers in history. He was at school with Mick Lunn, whose story begins on page 93. David remembers Mick well and Mick's father, Alf, and grandfather, William.

'William Lunn, who was famous in his own lifetime, looked just like James Robertson Justice when I first knew him. He had a big white beard and although he must have been pretty old by then he was still working on the river. But I worked for Alf, William's son, when I left school. I worked for about six years on the Houghton fishery with Alf before moving down to the Portsmouth Estate where I worked first for Lord Camrose. His fishing soon went to the Trenthams – a building family – but I stayed on.'

A jovial, fit-looking man with red hair and a rich Hampshire brogue, David retired in 1988 just a few months short of forty-two years as a full-time riverkeeper and gillie. When I went down to meet him I wondered why he'd left the Houghton fishery all those years ago.

'Well, I suppose I left to get on in the world. When I was at Houghton there were six riverkeepers and of course Mick Lunn, old Alfie's son, was always going to take over eventually. And it was exciting to move, particularly when I first got to Whitchurch in 1954, because I covered the Bourne and much more of the Test than in my last years. At the end I was looking after the 2½ miles of the Tufton Stretch. It was funny, too, in those early days – almost feudal. I can remember we were always bought two new 20oz tweed suits each year.'

The Tufton fishery, shallow throughout its length, is a picturesque and typical shallow chalkstream water, but it has its drawbacks. Weed-cutting, for example, is one of the most arduous tasks the chalkstream riverkeeper has to carry out and on the Tufton stretch it cannot be done from a boat, as David explained:

'Yes, all the weed-cutting had to be by hand simply because the water was so shallow – you just couldn't use chain-links or boats. Towards the end of my time I found the work too hard, but it was a good way to do it because doing it by hand is so selective. Using a 20ft pole with a scythe blade attached I'd cut neat rows across the river leaving 1yd gaps between the lines of weed.

'When you do this properly it keeps the water level up and the fish line up in the gaps like soldiers. It was old Alfie Lunn who taught me to cut weed. He always said you should cut to keep the water up and he was right. You cut bars and steps and in 200 or 300yd you should increase the depth by 2 or 3in and more water means a better flow and better fishing. When I started on the Tufton water we still irrigated the watermeadows in the old way. That was a real skill. Between one and three fields would always be under water right through the summer. The system was that there would always be one meadow under water, one drying out and one being used to feed stock. Flooding the meadows through the intricate system of hatches and sluices gave an excellent early growth of rich grass.

'Then one day this all stopped. A new farmer came – this was a good while ago mind – and all that work on the meadows finished. I thought it was very sad because it really was an art. I remember, too, that when a flooded field was being drained they even employed a man to go along and pick the fish out of the ditches. Lots of fish used to be left high and dry as the water was let back into the river and the meadow dried out.' Over the years David – known to all his fishing friends as 'Ginger' – taught an extraordinary range of people to fish. Everyone, in fact, from Lord Denning to racing driver Graham Hill. But teaching wasn't always easy.

'I remember trying to teach Lord Denning. It all started because he had a nephew who used to fish the river here. One day they both came down. He had one attempt at it and gave up immediately. He said the fish were too well educated for him.

'James Robertson Justice was a very keen fisherman who used to come here. I never had to give him a lesson. He was a nice man who lived at the Mill in Whitchurch, but he was always known in the village as the "Swear Man" because when he swore you really knew about it. You could hear him all over the village.

'Graham Hill, the racing driver, came down once with two friends. He picked it up very quickly and I can remember that chap who played Dr. Finlay coming down. He turned up with an old wicker creel and the first thing he said was "Come on, where are all the fish?" I've taught lots of different kinds of people over the years, many from America, lots of children and lots of women too. In my time I also taught three successive generations of one family.

'I remember many years ago teaching one young lady who would have been about fifteen at the time. Someone else had already tried to get her started without much success so I went to give a hand and soon she hooked and landed her first fish – a two-and-a-half-pounder. Afterwards the chap who'd earlier

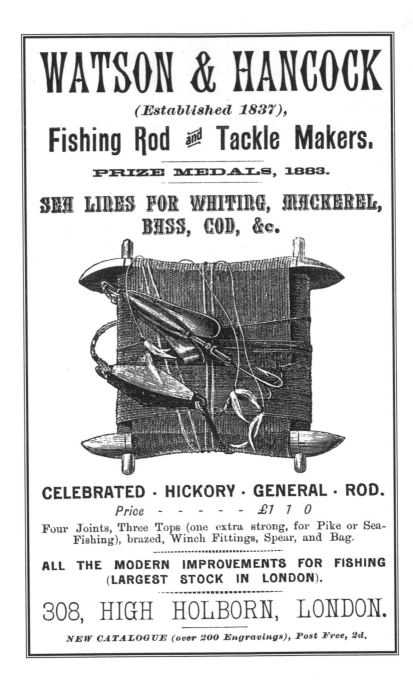

been trying to teach her said to me, "You treated her as if you were a sergeant-major." Well I suppose I probably did, but it worked,' said David with a broad grin.

'I think that, generally speaking, women pick up the skill of casting quicker than men, mainly because they are not so inclined to use brute force. Men tend to go at it like mad and then, of course, the fly drops uselessly on the water and they start cursing.

'But whoever it is, once you've helped them get a line out and they catch their first fish they are usually addicted. As a teacher you can have some fun too. I remember watching one man who just couldn't get his line out where he wanted it. So, to help, I cast his line out and quite by chance immediately hooked a fish. I don't think he thought much of that, but I gave the rod back to him with the fish still on. Another chap had been trying for a long time to cast under a bush on the far bank where a fish was lying. I tried for him and hooked the fish, but he absolutely refused to take the rod back and I had to play the fish. And some anglers are never satisfied whatever you do. I had to tell one chap that if he wanted to hook fish on the Tufton water he would have to strike more quickly because the water is so shallow. He didn't like being told that so he went to fish with Mick Lunn on the Houghton water further down and Mick had to tell him he was striking too slowly for their deeper water.'

The system on David's stretch of the Test was always to accompany anglers to the river and inevitably over the years he got to know his regular customers well. But his role as an instructor would continue long after his pupils had become proficient because regular fishermen often brought their guests along:

'I remember one old girl who came down with a friend who was a regular. She arrived in the middle of the day and started to fish, but she had terrible problems striking in time. What I used to do with all the people I taught was to shout "You" whenever I thought it was time for them to strike, but she never took any notice. Eventually I went and stood right behind her and when a fish rose to her fly I literally picked her up and ran backwards with her in my arms.

'It might sound a bit undignified, but she hooked that fish. And she didn't complain at all because she was so pleased she'd caught something. In fact she told me that that was the first fish she'd ever managed to hook.'

For David, work on the river had many highlights apart from the pleasure of introducing new people to fishing. And there were some supreme comic moments. Like the time he found an inflatable woman in the river.

'Oh yes we had a lot of fun with that. I fished her out of the river one day – I've no idea where she came from – and left her in the fishing hut, but with the legs just showing through the door. When my wife came down to the river to pick me up she saw it and got the fright of her life. She thought it was the bottom half of a dead body. After that we used to have a few jokes with it. I told one angler that his secretary was in the hut and sent him off to find the inflatable. Eventually I thought we'd had enough fun with her so I floated her off down the river to the next keeper.' Inevitably on a river there were wonderful tales of people falling in. David remembers one or two of these stories with particular relish:

'One young woman who came over from America to fish here with her father was casting from one of our bridges when a fish took her fly. We were all by the hut watching and just as she lifted the rod to hook the fish she stepped back straight into the river. We were so astonished that we were frozen to the spot. Mind you when she came up out of the water she still had her glasses on and she landed the fish.

'She had some excuse for falling in, but it's not always like that. I specifically told one man who was fishing in a tricky spot not to step back whatever happened and sure enough as soon as my back was turned he stepped straight into the river.'

David always enjoyed reminiscing about his years on the river, but he had mixed feelings about changes in fishing tackle and more particularly changes in the river environment.

'Tackle changed out of all recognition during my time. The old cane rods and gut casts went long ago, but I remember how difficult nylon was when it first came in. I remember an old riverkeeper at Stockbridge trying to learn to tie a fly on with nylon. He got in a terrible state because he'd been trying to tie his flies on with the old figure-of-eight knot. That was excellent for gut, but with nylon it just kept slipping.

'All the old boys down at Stockbridge used gut into the nylon era – this would be about the late fifties and early sixties – but there is no doubt that nylon is the better material. Apart from anything else it is stronger and thinner. General Sir Alan Cunningham was the last man to use gut on the Tufton water. He used it until the early 1970s and he died – still fishing at ninety-four. As I recall, he was a superb caster.

'In those far-off days the thing I really remember about tackle is that people were always moaning about hooks. Sometimes this made them strike as if their lives depended on it. One chap used to strike so hard that I told him any fish he hooked would end up half way across the field behind him.

'On the river, things changed greatly too. In my time we always had grids across the river. These held back all the weed when we started cutting and they also kept the fish in. These days boats go charging up and down the river and everyone has to cut at the same time. With the grids we could cut when we needed to. Some of the grids had already gone by the time I'd retired and it's only a matter of time before they are all gone. They used to keep the flow going too and thereby prevent silting up.

'We also used to net out the coarse fish. None of this modern electro-fishing nonsense. Netting is highly effective whereas with electro-fishing I don't think they got half the fish out. For pike we used to use a wire on an old stick. Snaring pike took a fair bit of skill because you'd have to sneak up on the old pike, get the wire round him and before he realised what was happening, whip him out.

'A lot of the changes I saw were based on money. It was just too expensive to devote the time and resources we used to devote to the river. When I first started we worked from eight in the morning till four in the afternoon during the week and at weekends we might work till midnight. But the era of the seven-day-a-week keeper has gone. And as the level of keepering has gone down so too has the fishing changed.

'It was much more put and take at the end of my time. In the 1970s and eighties two or three people would come to fish every day, but when I started people fished on only two or three days each week so the pressure on the river wasn't nearly so great. I remember a time when we could catch forty or fifty wild trout before lunchtime. Then there was a big pollution after the war and that killed the river. We gradually restocked it, but although the wild fish situation improved it'll never be as good as it was pre-war simply because of the pressure of the fishing.

'Another major disaster for us was the disease which struck in 1971. I picked out more than 500 dead fish during the winter of that year. They all had to be buried in quicklime or burnt.'

In his early days on the river, David always travelled around by bicycle, clearing the grids and checking the state of the water. While doing his rounds he was always bumping into other keepers and he believed that this helped reduce the amount of poaching.

'Oh, yes, it certainly did. In fact, since I retired there has been more poaching on the river than there was in the whole of my time. Mind you I did catch one poacher – and he got seven years.

'It all started when my wife and I spotted two men on the bank. I knew they were up to something so I called across to the local cowman and, with his dog, we ran towards the men. The dog wasn't much good because it only had one eye, but the poachers didn't know that and they tore off into the bushes. By this time the police had arrived. The poachers were caught but let off with a warning – they didn't take much notice though because a short while later they pinched some guns and did an armed robbery for which they got seven years. But I knew they'd had at least one of my fish. You see I knew every fish in the river and one big old brownie that had always been in the same place in the river had gone the day we caught them.'

Among the legitimate fishermen things were also changing dramatically. David can recall when everyone who fished at Tufton was glad that the mayfly had almost completely vanished.

'Yes, everyone was pleased about that in the fifties because mayfly time was known as duffers' fortnight. The skilful anglers at that time preferred to catch their trout on blue wings at the end of May and in the daytime. Personally I'm glad the mayfly came back, but they're strange insects and they do all disappear from particular areas now and then and it may take years for them gradually to make their way back up the river.'

The riverkeeper's life never made a man rich, but like other gillies and riverkeepers David was able to make a little additional money now and then. Particularly, as he told me, by trapping

eels. 'Most keepers had eel-traps along the river. We used to collect the eels during the last quarter of the old moon and the first
quarter of the new moon. And the eel fishing at Tufton was very
good. We used to catch about 3cwt of eels in a year.'

Fishing probably has more than its fair share of odd characters
and eccentrics and David met many during his long years on the
Test. 'I remember old Fred particularly. He was a real perfec-
tionist. He would even change his reel several times a day. Most
people change their flies a fair bit, but there aren't many who
worry too much about what reel they're using. He was also just
about blind when I knew him. I didn't realise this until one day
he gave me a lift in his car. We were driving along quite happily
when he suddenly asked me where we needed to turn. I told
him to make a right just after the next parked car. He said
"What car?" And it was right in front of us in broad daylight! I
used to have to tell him exactly where to cast, a yard up or a
yard down, but he was a good fisherman in spite of everything.
The last time he came down was the only blank day I think he
ever had. I thought that was rather sad so I gave him about two
dozen Morris Specials.'

The Morris Special is a superb fly invented by David to imi-
tate the blue upright and it has long been one of the most popular flies on the river. It bears witness to David's great
knowledge of the Test and its fish.

Looking after the river involved some activities that would be
frowned upon today, like getting rid of the swans. In his final
years David always liked to keep a pair on his stretch to keep all
the other swans away, but at one time the swans were shot. 'Too
many swans meant no weed so we used to shoot them. This was
long ago before they were protected, but I have to admit that
cygnet was delicious to eat and the feathers from the birds made
wonderful stuffing for the bolster.'

David's life was centred round some of the great old river-keeping characters. He still remembers Billy Beckenham, George Howell and Bill Taylor. All were keepers who spent their lives getting to know the river. David also knew Oliver Kite, one of the most famous fishermen this century.

'Oliver Kite died at Laverstock and I remember cycling to work the day it happened. I was pedalling along when I was suddenly stopped by my mate the local copper who asked me where I'd been earlier that morning because Oliver Kite had been found dead. Oliver had a stick with a notch cut in it for every fish he'd ever caught and when he was buried that stick was buried with him.

'Oliver was a great fisherman, but then there are always some people who just have a natural gift for it. You can always tell when someone is a natural. On my water we had a few, but we also had a few who never seemed to learn. At Tufton no one was supposed to cast until they'd seen a fish – mind you, some people, and it often seemed to be business people, never see a fish.

'There's a big class difference now too. At one time it was all very exclusive and I taught aristocrats and professional people. Towards the end of my time this changed completely and from one day to the next I could be helping people from all kinds of backgrounds.' After he retired David was presented with a river-keeper's long-service medal. The presentation was made by the Queen at the annual Game Fair. David was the first riverkeeper ever to receive this award.

THE ROYAL GILLIES

ALEC OGILVIE

After twenty-two years in the Argyll and Sutherland Highlanders, Alec Ogilvie heard rumours that the regiment was to be disbanded. As luck would have it, just when his future looked most uncertain (the regiment was actually saved in the end) he was offered what many fishermen would consider the top job in the gamefishing world: head-gillie to the Royal Family at Balmoral.

It was the regimental connection that put him in the right place at the right time.

'When the Royal Family used to arrive at Balmoral, certain regiments always came up to guard them. The Argyll and Sutherland Highlanders was always one of those regiments. While the soldiers are there they also act as beaters, ponymen and gillies. In fact, I started as a ponyman and gillie, having already been on duty there with the regiment.

'Depending on the season, gillies at Balmoral helped with all the sport: they accompanied guests to the hill and to the river.'

Alec's father was a keeper in Stirlingshire, but what tipped the balance in Alec's favour when the gillie's job first came up was probably the fact that he was also a piper.

'I used to play up at the house at the gillies' ball. Two of these were held. The first when the Queen and the rest of the Royal Family came up in September and the second at the end of October.

'On many estates the tradition is the same and the owners

would arrange a dance and a dinner for everyone who had helped with or been involved in the grouse shooting, salmon fishing or whatever. The Queen always attended the gillies' ball at Balmoral.

'The sovereign's own piper was always at the ball, but I also played – we wandered round the tables as the guests ate and drank and then played for them when they danced. It was mostly Scottish dancing, as you would expect, and the occasional quick-step. The Queen usually joined in.'

But fishing lay at the heart of Alec's work, particularly when the Queen Mother arrived with her party of guests in May:

'I gillied for her guests, but the Queen Mother was an expert and very experienced fisherwoman who knew the river very well under most conditions, so she didn't often need much help. Her guests tended to be friends and ex-employees. She used to stay for perhaps two or three weeks in May because that really was the best time of the year when most of the fish were caught. Like his grandmother, Prince Charles was also an expert, but then he had been coming here since he was a boy and he knew the river so well. I helped his guests too while he tended to go off on his own. And he caught some very good fish.'

Traditionally, the gillie had a very special place on any estate. Even where royalty was concerned the gillie was expected to tell the fisherman – or woman – where to fish and what fly to use. If they made a mistake he, the gillie, would be expected to put them right.

'A typical day for me started at about nine o'clock when I met the guests. I'd then take them down and show them the water. I'd show them where, depending on the conditions, the fish would be lying. I'd tie on their flies and, if necessary, show them how to fish a pool down. Most importantly, of course, I'd help when it came to playing a fish and netting it.'

There are three fishings at Balmoral: Abergeldy, Balmoral itself and Birkhall, where the Queen Mother fished. The total length of river is about 10 miles and, as this is the Dee, fishing starts on 1 February and continues until the end of September. Spinning was traditionally allowed at any height of water until 1 May, but after that date the rule was fly only unless the river rose to what Alec called the '2ft mark,' literally a white mark on a stone by the river.

Alec always argued that the most successful fly on the river Dee was the Monro Killer, although he himself took a thirty-pounder on a Devon minnow. 'Working as a gillie didn't reduce the fun of fishing for me and whenever I went down to the river I took a rod. When I caught my thirty-pounder I was using just 15lb line and I had to beach it alone – mind you even with that line I gave it some stick.'

Many people believe that the fishing at Balmoral is kept exclusively for the Royal Family. In fact much of it is let to people from all over the world. It is expensive – something that Alec didn't want to discuss – and if you want to fish in May you normally have to wait until someone dies. When that happens and a vacancy arises the fishing tends to go to those who have already been taking fishing earlier or later in the year. And there are the enormous attractions of Balmoral itself: houses on the estate are made available, for example, to some of those who come to fish. There are roughly ten pools on each beat, but some of these will be unfishable at different heights of water.

Things have changed greatly over the years and Alec watched and helped as anglers moved from the heavy greenheart and cane rods of his early years to the ultra-light carbon and boron rods in use today. But does everyone opt for space-age materials?

'Not at all. The Queen Mother still used a cane rod and Prince Charles never gave up cane and greenheart, which has a lovely soft action, although it's very heavy. In the old days everyone used 16 or 18ft greenheart rods in spite of the weight. And they did very well with them. In the thirties a forty-two-pounder was caught in Newton Pool on the Birkhall beat and many other thirty pounders were caught then. When the Queen Mother started fishing, rod sections were still spliced – literally lashed together with strips of leather.'

And there were other changes over the years. As tackle became lighter and stronger, the numbers of fish in the river decreased significantly:

'When I first came, the pools always seemed to be full of fish. Then deep-sea netting started and instead of taking hundreds of fish a year as we used to, the nets took hundreds of tons of fish. We bought the netting rights at the mouth of the Dee eventually, but of course that didn't stop the deep-sea netting. The fish ran the gauntlet from the Faroes to the river and then almost everywhere on the river itself.'

'We occasionally got poachers, too. I once spotted a blue van driving quickly away from the river and when I got down I noticed that the water in one pool was an odd, cloudy colour. Within minutes twenty-five salmon rose dead to the surface. We had the water tested and it had been poisoned with cyanide. Most of the poaching was much less serious, however.

'I once approached a laddie who had a great big bag of trout at his feet. He was upstream fishing with a worm. I asked him if he had a permit and he said no, but he knew the keeper well. I rather liked that answer because I'd never seen him before and I was the keeper he was referring to.'

When the fishing ended each September Alec didn't simply hang up his rods and wait for the next season. He helped feed the deer out on the hill and tended the banks of the river until the first fishermen arrived the following spring.

'I was never able to imagine doing anything else. I'm near my family and although I was always busy on the river the job had great attractions of peace and quiet. You saw an enormous amount of wildlife – everything from otters and peregrine falcons to golden eagles – and you had the chance to live in a beautiful place just two minutes' walk from the river.

JIM EWAN

Jim Ewan, who was born in 1936, was the closest of all the Balmoral gillies to the Queen Mother. A mild-mannered and self-deprecating man, Jim lived in a remote cottage about 6 miles from the main house at Balmoral. He was a gillie for more than thirty years and for most of the 1980s he looked after the Queen Mother personally when she came up to fish.

'The Queen Mother normally came in May, usually a very good time on the Dee so she kept the whole month, but she might only stay herself for ten days or a fortnight.'

Jim's first job at Balmoral was as a stalker, and being out on the hill taught him the skills and diplomacy necessary for dealing with estate guests, whether they were there to shoot or fish. 'I'd been a stalker for nearly twenty years when the job of fishergillie came up and although I took the job I still kept up my connection with the shooting.'

Jim's connection was, in fact, limited to helping with the pheasant shooting which was organised on a fairly small-scale basis and, as with the fishing, it was organised for the Queen Mother. 'We had a good stock of wild birds, but we never had big days, days when a lot of birds are shot. The Queen Mother and her guests just came to enjoy what was really only a bit of rough shooting. We just worked through the root fields and we might shoot about fifty birds in a day. But the Queen Mother's great love was fishing.'

Jim explained to me that although most of his work as a fisher-gillie involved accompanying the fishermen and women down to the river they didn't all need the same amount of attention:

'Well the first thing that has to be said is that it was never a difficult job gillying for the Queen Mother herself. She tended to get on with her fishing and I helped only when the conditions were particularly difficult or when we were trying to winkle out a particular fish. She really knew the ins and outs of the river, but I sometimes did a little more for her friends. They sometimes needed extra help.'

No mean fisherman himself Jim landed several salmon over 20lb 'some were on the fly, but most, I'm afraid, were caught spinning' he confessed with a chuckle. Jim is a neat, compact man with a full head of strikingly white hair and a surprisingly young-looking face. Like all the Royal gillies, he always had a quiet admiration for those members of the Royal Family for whom he worked.

'Prince Charles was an excellent fisherman and like his grandmother he was a traditionalist. I know they both like the traditional feel of older rods rather than the latest carbon fibre or boron.

'I've landed fish up to about 10lb for the Queen Mother, but we always knew there was the chance of a really big fish during May when she was fishing. In fact, one of her guests lost a very good fish a couple many years ago after playing it for more than two hours – that was on a fly and I think that fish must have weighed more than 30lb.'

In spite of the fact that he didn't come from a family of fishermen, Jim clearly enjoyed his time as a gillie. 'Well if you enjoy the countryside and wildlife, not to mention a working life that is mostly spent out of doors, gillying is a great life. It's also got plenty of variety. In my time here, for example, I've worked on all the royal beats of the Dee – Abergeldy, Balmoral itself and now Birkhall where we have two rods fishing at any one time. I've enjoyed every moment of it.'

Jim may have enjoyed it all, but there was a note of sadness in his voice when he explained that 1989 was the first year he could ever remember when the Queen Mother did not actually fish the river at all.

'Well she came down as usual, but this is the first time she didn't even attempt to fish. She watched the others fishing and kept an eye on things generally, but she didn't have a cast.'

CHARLIE WRIGHT

Charlie Wright was born in the village of Braemar where Robert Louis Stevenson wrote *Treasure Island*. Braemar is also the nearest village to the main house at Balmoral where Charlie worked for some forty years. He always refused to give his exact age, but admitted to being almost as old as the century and even when he retired he still occasionally helped with the gillying on the Balmoral beat.

'In a way I was on the river for the whole of my life because I was born just a stone's throw from it. I've gillied for Prince Charles in my time, but he tends to fish at Birkhall with the Queen Mother. Like me, the Prince uses an old greenheart rod – greenheart is a marvellous material for a rod because it will almost fish itself. Certainly, it's heavy, but it has a lovely soft action which is much better than anything you'll get with these new carbon-fibre rods. In the old days everyone used greenheart and cane and they didn't have any problems, so there's no real reason why using greenheart should be a problem today.

'The main problem with fibreglass and carbon rods is that they take a very long time to subdue a fish. I've always fished with greenheart and I've landed fish to 27½lb on it. I also use a cane rod but nothing can really beat greenheart.

'Most of the people I took out on the river over the years were friendly enough, but there is a huge social divide between a gillie and the man or woman he helps. It's silly to pretend otherwise, but then fishing is unlike any other sport in that it's a highly social affair. Fishing puts people in a good mood, generally speaking (and especially after they land a good fish) although after a few drams we often had people falling into the river, or getting hooked up on trees and rocks. I always felt it was my role to calm the fraught situation and get the angler back doing what he was supposed to be doing – fishing.'

SOMETHING
OF A DIPLOMAT

_____ ooooo _____

'W hen I came here in 1961 my heart sank. I'd seen an advertisement in the local paper for the job of assistant riverkeeper and I thought it sounded marvellous, but when I got here there were at least forty other lads waiting to be interviewed. I thought to myself – you've had it with this one.'

Tony Waites needn't have worried. He told his future employer that he wanted the job to make something of his life. That clinched it and he became assistant keeper on the most famous chalkstream water outside the South of England: the Driffield Anglers' Club water on the Driffield Beck in East Yorkshire.

In those early years Tony worked with Bill Burn who'd started his career on the Test and it wasn't until the late sixties that Tony finally took over as headkeeper. 'Well, ironically, it was after I fell out with the place really. I left for a year in 1967 and worked in a factory. It was just that I didn't like the way Bill worked. I went to work in a factory where I made a lot more money. I got married at that time too, but then, out of the blue, the club approached me and asked if I would come back as headkeeper. So I sold my house – I made £50 profit on it – and came back to Poundsworth where I've been ever since.'

Tony wasn't a typically bluff Yorkshireman, but a cheerful, down-to-earth, ruddy-faced chap who looked as strong as a horse and probably was. He was born just 3 miles from the river where he spent most of his working life – in fact he enjoyed an early, if slightly dubious, relationship with the river.

'Oh yes. I was caught poaching when I was about nine. I'd taken ten trout – they were all over 3lb, and I'd tickled them out of the river. Tickling trout is a real skill. You have to be as steady as anything, get your hand underneath the fish while he's lying there under the bank and then quick as you can whip him out. The stupid thing is I didn't even like eating trout – my dad didn't either. He was strictly a meat man so he buried the trout and said, with great disgust, "We don't eat stuff like that.".'

The Driffield Anglers' Club was formed in 1833 and although the clubhouse – above which Tony lived – is a relatively new building it contains a wealth of old cased fish caught by club members, detailed records of the fishery, a beautiful early long-case clock and a plaque which lists all the past presidents of the club – except one: 'Yes that gap in the list is there because we just don't know who the first president was, but in 1835 a chap called Harrington Hudson became president and his great-great-grandson, was still a member in my time. So that gives you some idea of the continuity the club has been able to achieve.'

Like many chalkstream clubs, Driffield was always pretty exclusive, but less so as time went on, as Tony explained.

'When I started out there were just twenty-five members, but that number had reached thirty-six twenty years later and of course many of the members' wives also enjoyed fishing. That was sometimes a bit of a problem because we only had a gents' loo.

'The members were a real mix – we had farmers, solicitors, surgeons, judges and old colonels. And most of them seemed extremely ancient to me. I don't think anybody was ever in a great hurry about joining either – there was always a twenty-year waiting list! And you could only get in if an existing member nominated you. This had to be followed by a seconder and then your name went into a hat. If anyone at all objected then you didn't get in. It was as simple as that.

'The club was always in a slightly difficult position, too, because it never actually owned anything. All its water was rented from riparian owners and, of course, that meant the price went up every year.'

Tony was employed as a riverkeeper, but he did a great deal of what would usually be called gillying: 'I went out every day with the fishermen. I put their flies on the end of their lines and told them which flies to use according to the conditions, time of year and so on. Many of our members didn't know how to tie a fly on. I also tied flies for the members. And they were a mean lot sometimes. They thought they could have my flies for nothing!'

Any criticisms Tony may have had of his clients' foibles were always expressed with a smile and he was clearly devoted to the river and to the club:

'I never went anywhere. I was always happy just to stay by the river. I don't think I ever even went on holiday with my children! I know that sounds terrible, but I didn't like going away or meeting people and I could never stand parties. I used to get a month off each year, but I never took it as holiday. I just had the odd day here and there. When I was at work I was almost always in bed by nine-thirty. People thought I was a bore – I suppose I was in a way, but that's what gillying and riverkeeping did to me. They got into my blood.

'People in the know used to say that gillying was a twenty-nine-hour-a-day job. I used to get up at about five and drive straight down to the bottom beat. I had 9 miles of river to cover, keeping a lookout for poachers and vandals. And I was always a nosy bugger – I always wanted to know exactly who was fishing. But with me being on the river so much my wife used to play

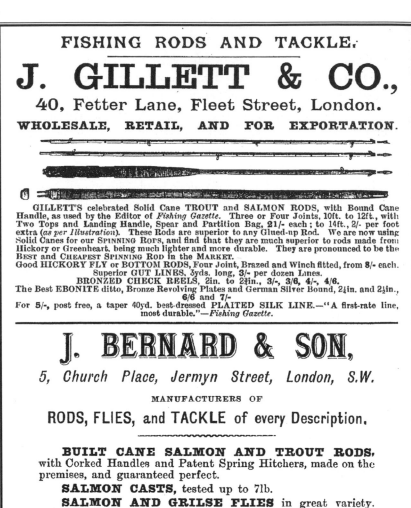

hell with me, she didn't even sleep with me some nights!'

Hoots of laughter from Tony, who obviously took life's troubles in his stride. It was difficult to know when he was being entirely serious, such was his glee at any story to do with his life on the river. He was particularly entertaining when he described his relationship with club members.

'Lots of our members didn't fish at all – and that's saying something when you've only got thirty-six anyway. Our president didn't even fish, and although he was very old the fact that he didn't fish had nothing to do with his age. In thirty years I never saw him with a rod in his hand. Don't ask me why because I just don't know.

'Each year the members used to invite me to their big dinner for a drink. They even used to drink a toast to me, but I never got invited to the meal itself. I used to call them all 'Sir' and they all called me Tony, except the president who called me Waites. Mind you the members used to treat me very well, although I had to be something of a diplomat because with some of the insider information I used to get from the members – and I'm not going to tell you which ones – I could have made a fortune on the Stock Exchange. I also used to get some very good racing tips.

'The average number of days fished by each member was probably only about nine per season, but that's no bad thing because it means less pressure on the river. Most of the members were locals, but we used to have a number of rich steelmen from Sheffield. They kept the club going when nobody else had any money. There were four or five keepers in victorian times – in my day it was just me and an assistant. We needed more keepers at one time because we had the canal and a lot more of the river – nearly 20 miles in fact. The canal used to be very good. In the late 1880s it produced a wild trout of about 19lb.

'When I took over here the trout were averaging 12–14oz and

that low average may have had something to do with the fact that the river was stuffed with pike. I took out seventy-six in one week on a stretch just ½ mile long. They were good pike too. I remember we had one of about 13lb.

'After we got rid of the pike we started to get some good trout, including a wild brownie of 6½lb. We didn't stock with big fish bought in, but I'd usually rear and release about four hundred brown trout and about two hundred rainbows each year.

'The fishing was organised on a beat system. We once tried doing it by picking names out of a hat and allocating them to a beat that way, but it didn't work very well so we went back to the old way. The members used to sit around the club table in the morning and decide where they were going to go. It was all done in a good-natured way. They just worked it out among themselves. We had ten beats in all and the rod limit for the day was three brace. It used to be four brace, but I reduced it – no one needs to take that many fish in a day.

'I didn't fish much myself in those days, but I'd always sneak in a few goes when the members were having lunch. And I always used their tackle. I never owned a proper rod myself. I'd been given plenty over the years, but I always gave them away. My old boss James Young – he was the stream manager – once told me to go and get a gun and a dog and he would pay for them. But, generally speaking, I used to prefer to watch and see what was happening on the river. It's easy to get too obsessed with catching fish. Early on, of course, I was like that. I wanted to catch as many as I could and then I wanted to catch huge individual specimens, but you get over all that.'

Like most riverkeepers and gillies, Tony believed that fishing and eccentricity went hand in hand and he has some marvellous, but entirely libellous stories of various people's angling escapades. One in particular he was prepared to repeat to me.

'One day a long time ago I was just wandering down the river to see one of our older members – he's dead now – who was fishing what we call The Island. I reached the river but I just couldn't find him anywhere. Then, out of the corner of my eye, I spotted his big Jaguar parked over by one of our sheds. When I got over to the car, there he was sitting on the ground stark naked. He had a gin and tonic in one hand and just said "Tony, I've lost my bloody sunglasses."

'Apparently he'd slipped while fishing a spot where there was a very steep bank and gone right into the river head over heels. He'd taken off all his clothes, strung his fly line between the Jag and a nearby tree, and hung his gear up to dry.

'It was one of the funniest things I've ever seen because he was about 6ft 9in tall and we didn't find his glasses for two years, by which time he was dead anyway.'

Tony chuckled to himself throughout this story, which he admitted he has been dining out on for years. And as the years have passed Tony has learned a great deal, both about the ways of the fishermen and the trout. One of his greatest pleasures was always teaching: 'One of the best things about this job is that you get to teach the kids. I love children and I taught many of our members when they were children. Then they grew up, married and started to bring *their* children down to learn to fish.'

The Driffield Beck had one great disadvantage, compared at least to most chalkstreams in the South of England. It had lost virtually all its insect life.

'We used to have a good hatch of mayfly here, but that was long before my time. I never saw a mayfly here. I think the dredging put paid to the mayfly. The dredging eventually stopped and we even tried releasing mayfly, but it never came to anything. Still someone is bound to have another go at some time. In theory it should be possible to re-introduce them.'

Perhaps the highlight of Tony's career was an invitation to a special dinner held in London by the Fly Fishers' Club in 1985. But as Tony recalls, it was a night of mixed blessings:

'Well it was a big thing for me to go to that dinner. I hate London and I hate dressing up – I had to hire a bloody dinner-jacket for that do. Anyway it was held at the Savoy and three hundred people turned up to eat bangers and mash together. I loved the Fly Fishers' Club itself. They told me afterwards that I was the first person in about ten years to ask to have a look at their library.

'At the end of the dinner I was completely paralytic – I'd never had so many gin and tonics in my life, but it was quite an experience. I remember the president of the Fly Fishers came up to me and said, "What the bloody hell are you doing here?" He was only kidding because he'd fished with me a few weeks earlier.'

Tony used to fish with the Princess of Wales' mother, Mrs Shand Kidd, 'she had supper with us as well,' and with the great Oliver Kite: 'Oliver Kite was a marvellous man. I only met him for one afternoon, but he showed me how to tie a Kite's Imperial and he did a bit of fishing with us.'

The only subject that seriously dampened Tony's enthusiasm was vandalism. But surely poaching must have been a bigger headache? 'Not at all. Our big worry was always vandals. I don't know why it was, but people thought they could go anywhere and do anything they liked. I used to spend a lot of time looking after the banks, building and repairing seats and bridges and then some bugger would come along and start smashing things up. They seemed particularly fond of throwing our seats in the river. Seats also got stolen – I'd put them out one day and the next morning they were gone. The real problem was that there were new housing developments around here and I think the kids just got bored.'

In spite of the fact that Driffield is a long way north of more traditional chalkstream country, its season doesn't differ much from its brother rivers in the South Country. 'We started on the first Monday of May and fished till the end of October for rainbows and until the end of September for the browns,' explained Tony.

I walked the banks with Tony and his friend, the photographer Roy Shaw who spent decades fishing and photographing the river. Both men were clearly devoted to it and it did indeed look lovely as it wandered through farmland and rich woodland. Tony was utterly convinced that the life of the riverkeeper was unbeatable. He did, however, admit that there were drawbacks:

'There was never any money in the riverkeeping lark. At Christmas I did quite well, but the tips here could be pretty awful and even when they were generous it was not always the wealthiest who gave the most. You tended to get better tips from the older ones. Mind you, one old chap gave me £2 in an envelope every Christmas for more than twenty years – I used to wonder if he'd ever heard of inflation!

'The tipping tradition was definitely dying out, which was a pity really because we did a lot for the fishermen – everything in fact from gillying for them to making tea and freezing and smoking their fish.'

THE
Experienc'd
Angler;
or
Angling
Improved.

Sold by Rich: Marriott in St. Dunstans Church yard
Vaughan sculp.

A METICULOUS
RECORDER OF LIFE

─────────── ooooo ───────────

Allan Cooke, now in his seventies, enjoyed the rare distinction of having worked with the great Frank Sawyer, whose book, *Nymphs and the Trout*, was and is one of the classics of angling literature. Allan took over from Frank, but they had already been friends and colleagues for many years by then. Both men spent their lives working on the Upper Avon at Netheravon, Wiltshire.

'My mother and father went to school with Frank Sawyer,' recalled Allan. That would have been about 1915–20. Frank took the riverkeeper's job here on the Services Dry Fly Fishing Association water in 1928 and he continued with it until I took over from him in the sixties.

'I reckon I really got the job through my uncle. He'd worked with Frank part time since 1948. I suppose that, in truth, I started on the river, helping with the weed-cutting and so on, when I was about thirteen. 'When I left school I drifted away from riverkeeping for a few years. I started work on a farm, although I carried on with odd jobs down on the river. Then I worked as a printer for the RAF. I don't know why, but I soon decided that the riverkeeper's life was for me. I suppose it was in my blood really, what with having so many family connections with the river. What really got me back was Frank Sawyer, who just said to me out of the blue one day "You don't want a job on the river I suppose?" I told him I'd think about it, so I did. Having thought about it, I turned up for the job.

'Frank Sawyer was all right, but a lot of people couldn't get on with him at all. He was a very abrupt sort of character – mind you, a lot of what he said was true and a lot of people didn't like that either.

'He was old before his time was Frank, and we did have cross words now and then. He gradually got slower and slower and then one day I found him dead down by the river. I'd gone down with the dog after lunch and I was just behind Netheravon Church. His wife had asked me to go look for him because she hadn't seen him for a while. When I found him he was flat out with his walking stick still in his hand. My uncle, who'd worked with Frank all those years, was also found dead on the riverbank. I remember that very well. We were putting in a post together and he said he had to go and get a shovel. He set off and he never came back. Frank Sawyer was the one who taught me to fish and he gave his favourite rod to my uncle. My uncle kept a diary all about the river and his life on it for forty-five years, but his wife burned the lot when he died. A terrible waste. Diaries seem to be all the rage among riverkeepers. I suppose it's because it's a contemplative sort of job – I kept a diary from my earliest days. I used to record parish events, how the river was fishing, how my bees were doing and so on.

'Although this was the Services Club we didn't just get military people. There were civilians as well as serving and retired officers. We had a total of one hundred members, including any number of knights and generals.

'Many were in their eighties. We even had the Governor of the Falklands here to fish once.

'The Services Club started in 1898 when the estates round about were bought by the ministry. Soon after that the club was founded. Records go back to the twenties and from them you can see that it was originally called the Officer's Fishing Association. These days the men – the ordinary soldiers – fish as well.'

A slight figure, Allan had a quiet but intense manner and he was a meticulous recorder of life in and around Upavon. His talk, like his diaries, always returned to the life of the river.

'Poaching was always a bit up and down – more one year less the next – but the important thing was that we should be able to keep it at a tolerable level.

'It has to be said, too, that in their young days my uncle and Frank Sawyer used to do a bit of poaching. But this was for pike in the early twenties. They used to go down to Milston where they knew the riverkeeper would turn a blind eye. They used spears, wire, treble hooks, you name it, but the pike are a nuisance when you're trying to preserve the trout so I suppose they were really doing the keeper a favour, although strictly speaking they shouldn't have been on the river at all.

'Frank used to use what we call a turnbuckle spear. It probably sounds a bit cruel now, but it was made with a sharpened brass cartridge case and a tough piece of wire. Basically the cartridge case was so sharp you could stab it through the pike's body as it hovered in the water perhaps under a bank somewhere, and the wires would grip the fish long enough for you to whip it out. Sounds a bit cruel, but if you've got to get them out what else can you do?

'The other technique we used for pike was a wire noose on a pole. It takes a lot of skill to lower a noose like this over an unsuspecting pike's head and then flip him out on to the bank. I remember once we used Frank's walking stick with a wire on it and the fish escaped with the stick. It was hilarious, although Frank didn't really think so. You could see it sticking up out of the water and weaving its way downstream.

'The poaching of single fish wasn't a problem here. It was the

Plate 1.

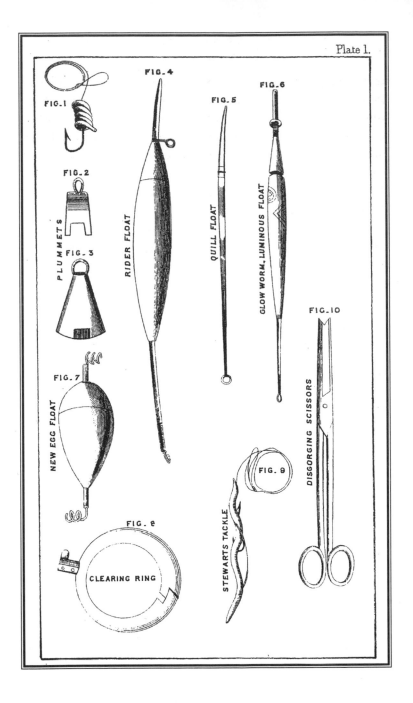

FIG. 1

FIG. 2

PLUMMETS

FIG. 3

FIG. 4

RIDER FLOAT

FIG. 5

QUILL FLOAT

FIG. 6

GLOW WORM, LUMINOUS FLOAT

FIG. 7

NEW EGG FLOAT

FIG. 8

CLEARING RING

FIG. 9

STEWARTS TACKLE

FIG. 10

DISGORGING SCISSORS

stewponds you had to watch. Seven miles of river was a lot to
keep a regular watch on and even if you did catch someone they
were sometimes pretty nasty. I remember stopping one poacher
who suddenly turned round and attacked me with a knife.
Luckily, before I was injured someone else came along. Other
poachers who've got as far as the courts have threatened to beat
me up, but Frank had all these problems in his day. In fact, during the war Frank had to try to catch poachers who used gelig-
nite to blow the fish out of the water.'

Rearing trout for release in the river was one of Allan's most
important jobs, but where necessary he also helped newcomers
to the water, showing them how to cast into difficult places and
where fish were lying:

'Normally they rang me if they needed anything, but most of
my time was spent either catching the trout and stripping them
of their eggs or working at the one hundred and one tasks fish
rearing also involves. We didn't release very small fish every
year, but we might release as many as twenty thousand fry
some years.

'Frank Sawyer started the rearing and release policy in 1935.
He built the first hatchery and we carried on from there. I used
to put in about one thousand takeable fish – that's about 1in
long – in April and then another five hundred in July.'

The stocking policy on Allan's water might seem high but, as
he pointed out, the Avon just could not sustain a sufficient wild
stock to cope with the pressures of fishing and pollution.

'The pollution we got as a result of run-off from the roads and
fields always seemed to come at the worst time – when the fish
were trying to breed. All those chemicals used to affect the ova
– in fact they damaged the whole ecology of the river. There
were times when things seemed a little better, but generally
speaking the river and its water quality deteriorated massively

over the years. I was always convinced that one of the biggest problems was the salt they used on the roads. In this area it killed massive beech trees, so I hate to think what it did to the delicate life of the river.

'We also suffered the disturbance caused by too many visitors. It's wasn't just fishermen. It was walkers, ramblers and all the associated beer cans and polystyrene and other rubbish that got chucked in the river.'

Allan's water was always primarily brown trout fishing, but he did experiment briefly and unsuccessfully with rainbows. 'They were detrimental to the brownies,' he says.

He never took a holiday and he spent virtually all his time on the river from early morning, when he checked his fish ponds, till late at night. It was a life of constant attention, but there were lighter moments when he managed to get down to the river to fish or to help others. Levels of ability among the Services' anglers varied enormously:

'One or two old fellows never seemed to know what they wanted to do when they got down here. Some could never catch a thing. They carried their rods as if they were on a route march and it was impossible to get them to understand that two thirds of the battle with dry fly fishing is to wait and watch. If they'd bothered to keep a close eye on the river they'd have seen plenty of fish to cast to, but they were always busy moving about and talking to each other.

'If you're storming along the bank the whole time you'll scare every fish in the vicinity. I remember following one chap along the bank for about two miles. He was going as fast as his legs would carry him and then at the end of the day he came up to me and said he'd caught nothing. I told him that I'd watched him and that I'd hardly been able to keep up with him. If he'd slowed down a bit he might have caught something or at least seen a fish.'

Allan's career spanned all the momentous changes in fishing tackle and he was particularly pleased that Frank Sawyer also managed to live into the era of lighter, modern fishing rods. 'Frank might have been a lifelong devotee of cane, but I remember driving him down to Southampton to collect some of the very first carbon rods to arrive in Britain. The one thing he didn't like about carbon was that it made the manufacturers believe they could make one rod for all purposes. Old Frank wouldn't have any of that.'

Allan kept a rod given to him by Frank Sawyer. 'Yes, he won that rod in France. It's wonderful to have it but I never used it much myself – I was always too busy working on the river, but that was as much fun as fishing.

'Once they were fully paid-up, members were allowed to fish as often as they liked, but I'm not sure that was such a good thing with all the extra pressure it brought. I think in some ways it was better in the old days when no fishing was ever allowed on a Monday. That gave the fish a rest. There were never many coarse fish in the river, but now and then there was a bit of excitement when one of the members caught a giant roach on a fly. I remember one chap had a roach over 2lb.'

Allan's water included a special area where local children were allowed to fish free of charge, but even this had its problems: 'The kids used to take some good fish, but we didn't mind. A lot of them were good little fishermen and they'd put some of their fish back, but of course you always got a few little blighters who'd take a wheelbarrow load home if they could get away with it.'

BATTLES WITH
THE POACHERS

――――――― ⚬⚬⚬⚬⚬ ―――――――

G ordon Rogers looked after more than 20 miles of the
Upper Taw as it crosses the wilds of Dartmoor. He
worked on the river for more than thirty years and
earned a long-service award from his last employer, the old
National Rivers Authority (NRA). Keepering, of one sort or
another, had been in the Rogers family for a long time.

'Well I started work as a riverkeeper in the late 1950s. I was
employed at that time by the North Devon River Board which
eventually became the pollution watchdog, the NRA. But my
family had worked for the Poltmores for three generations. My
father and grandfather were gamekeepers for Lord Poltmore and
I originally worked as a gardener for the family. I was there for
eighteen years, but then Lord and Lady Poltmore went to South
Africa. That was why I became a riverkeeper, but I think
keepering is in our blood.

'When I started I looked after the Upper Taw and the Mole
and the Bray. On the Taw we got salmon and sea trout early in
March. These fish moved right up the river as far as North
Taunton. The rest of the fishing was mostly brown trout, but
someone occasionally caught an escapee rainbow.

'Our big problem down here was gang poaching – in fact it
was almost gang warfare. The Bridport Gang was the main one
with about forty members, but they were always very crafty and
difficult to catch. They used to net the river in twos and threes

and with the river crossing much of the most remote bit of Dartmoor it was always an uphill task for the riverkeeper. With the help of the police we did catch them now and then, but you wouldn't want to tackle them on your own. One of our bailiffs tried that when he caught two men poaching on the Mole and they beat him up so badly he was off work for a week. It's ridiculous, but the police wouldn't prosecute the two men. Apparently there was insufficient evidence – in other words it was just the bailiff's word against that of the poachers.'

A small bespectacled figure, Gordon was philosophical about the problems he faced from the poachers. He took the view that poaching could never be entirely stamped out, but that it could at least be kept to a minimum. His only other big worry was pollution and of his three successive employers, first the North Devon River Board, then the South West Water Authority and finally the National Rivers Authority, the NRA was, he believes, in the strongest position to stop the polluters:

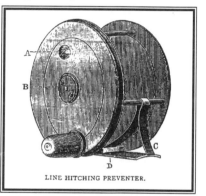

LINE HITCHING PREVENTER.

'The NRA could have worked well now because at the time everyone was that bit more conscious of green issues and the dangers of pollution. I think the problem was that it never really had sufficient backing. My main task, so far as pollution was concerned, was to police the farms along the Taw. The hill farmers were pretty Good – only a small percentage were breaking the law. Our system was to classify farms in three ways: if they were polluting the river we classified them as red; if they looked as if they might cause problems we classed them as green. The final category – blue – meant that a farm was OK so far as pollution was concerned.

'If a farm was green, if it looked as if it might cause trouble, we sent in advisors to tell the farmer what he needed to do to put the situation right. Out of seventy-seven farms we visited on a typical survey, sixty-five were blue, nine green and three red. I didn't think that was too bad, but we were lucky. We didn't have the dairy herds – they were what really caused trouble because with dairy herds you get silage and slurry. We looked to see if a farm was producing too much slurry or if sheep dips were sited in silly places or if the drainage system was not all that it should be.

'We gave offending farms a time limit to clean up and if they sorted things out in that time we didn't prosecute. A few big farms on the Taw were still running risks so we kept an eye on them, but the Taw was nowhere near as bad as the Torridge which had a terrible time with pollution.'

I was talking to Gordon in his neat little cottage in the heart of the Devon village of South Molton, where he was born in 1927. Things changed enormously in the West Country in his time, as he explained.

'Well, take poaching. In my early days people didn't come into the area from outside to poach. We were to some extent a more closed community because there were no motorways and so on. The only poachers were the local farmers. They used to use pitchforks to stab the fish on the shallows. If you looked along the river some nights it was like Blackpool illuminations because each farmer used a torch to spot the fish and there were farmers all along some stretches.

'In those days it was fairly easy and cheap to get a ticket to fish legally. That all changed towards the end of my time as wealthier people came in and bought up the fishing rights. I only just managed to get a beat for myself on the middle Taw. First time I fished I got two salmon in a morning, then nothing for the rest of the season.

'When I first worked on the river I did a lot more gillying. All the fishermen in those days were what I suppose you would call gentlemen – twenty years later it had all changed and we had the dustman, the coalman, schoolteachers, everyone, which was a good thing I think. I remember one doctor who needed some help to land his sixth fish of the day. I tailed it for him and then he asked me if I would help him carry it back along the river. I don't think he would have managed without me, but when we got back to his car he offered me the pick of the six fish. A lot of anglers were very generous like that. I tailed an eighteen-pounder for another angler. He then took it back to his hotel, had it cleaned and gave me half.

'A typical day for me used to start at about eight o'clock when I checked the river at the different bridges. I would see what sort of fly life was about, check the colour of the water, the temperature and the flow rate. I might then wander along to see who was fishing. At the famous Junction Pool I always used to notice that on a Monday the anglers would often be swaying from side to side as they stood on the bank: the reason was that they'd had a good session the night before in the hotel bar!

'Later in the day I'd check anglers' licences, check for any obstructions in the river and, of course, keep an eye out for signs of pollution. We were always on a twenty-four hour alert, but I usually got home by five or six in the evening. When the sea trout started to run from June on I was often out all night, but you've really got to know your water if you're patrolling at night. You can't use a torch because every poacher will then see you from miles away.

'The record salmon for the Taw weighed about 32lb. It was

caught at Waterburn by a Mr Owen a long time ago. It's a record that's unlikely to be beaten because there's too much high-seas netting, too much disease and too much angling pressure. We did once find a massive cock salmon dead – in condition that fish would probably have weighed 40lb.

'A ¾lb trout is a good fish these days, but we do occasionally get a wild three-pounder – I remember my brother-in-law caught an absolute beauty just over 3lb about thirty years ago. Fish that size were few and far between.

'Down here we used to fish from 1 March to 30 September, with spinning for salmon allowed in March and April only. After that it was fly only. I usually managed to fish on one or two days

a week right through the season. I didn't get my fishing because I worked on the river – that didn't in itself entitle me to fish anywhere, but I always managed to secure a private bit of water here and there.

'Before all the nitrates and detergents and the UDN disease I can remember hooking five salmon in one morning – mind you I lost all five! I said to myself after that, if I lose one more fish I'm going to pack up and go home. I hooked two more in fact and landed both. My only other claim to fame is that I hold the record for the biggest rainbow trout ever caught in Westlandpound Reservoir. I caught it on an Appetiser and it weighed 13lb 2½oz.

'I was a keen fly tier and did a bit of shooting now and then, but I could never get too involved in other things because I never knew when I might be called out in an emergency. The police regularly called me out of bed at three in the morning because a gang of poachers had been spotted on the Taw. We had to sneak up on them in the darkness and then wait for first light. When they saw us they'd make a run for it, but we usually managed to catch them, including one chap who tried to swim across the river. We let ten good salmon go one night.

'I always used a 17ft carbon rod, but some of the anglers down here still used cane into the 1970s and eighties and one chap still used a massive greenheart rod – and he caught fish on it – when I retired. The Dartmoor rivers became better known during my time, particularly as salmon fishing became more and more popular; in fact towards the end we had regular visits from German, Dutch and American fishermen.

'It's odd though, because my strongest memory of all my years working on the river doesn't really have anything to do with fishing. I was out late one evening down by one of the bridges over the Taw when I heard this strange whistling noise.

I couldn't think what it was and then, coming along the river towards me, I saw an otter carrying a baby otter in its mouth. I watched in complete astonishment for quite a time until it disappeared. I don't know how rare it is to see something like that, but I will never forget it. And I don't think I'll ever see anything like it again because although there are a few otters left their numbers are much lower than in years past.'

Gordon Rogers died in October 1992.

ENCHANTED
BY THE RIVER

──────── ooooo ────────

J im 'the fish' Smith worked for nearly forty years on the 20-odd miles of the Sussex Ouse owned by the Ouse Angling Preservation Society which was founded in 1875. Jim was in a unique position among riverkeepers because he looked after a river that was and is both an important coarse fishery and a game fishery. Famed for its giant chub and roach, the Sussex Ouse is also one of the very few rivers of any importance for big sea trout in the South East.

Jim was a marvellously avuncular man with a delightful Sussex drawl and with the ideal temperament – tolerant, friendly and helpful – for a most difficult job. He was born just a few miles from where he spent most of his life in the tiny village of Isfield. His father was a carter in the days before the coming of the motor car and when Jim left school he started work as a cottage gardener for Lord Rupert Neville. The estate was sold soon after Jim started work and the land is now – always to Jim's great regret – a massive housing estate.

Already a keen fisherman, he was approached by the secretary of the Ouse Angling Preservation Society soon after he left school and asked if he would like to take over as riverkeeper. I wondered if the offer had come as a surprise. 'Good heavens no. I'd fished since I was a little boy and I fished here on the Ouse from the time I was six. The job was ideal and after I started I never thought of doing anything else. The job was particularly

THE ANGLER'S DREAM

LISTEN TO THE ANGLER'S DREAM! —
HE DREAMS THAT HE IS BY A STREAM,
TALKING TO A LOVELY BREAM;
BY HIS SIDE RECLINES A CARP,
PLAYING TUNES UPON A HARP;
WHILE A DACE
DRESSED IN LACE
SINGS THE VERY DEEPEST BASS.

THROUGH THE TREES HE SEES A PERCH
KNEELING IN THE VILLAGE CHURCH,
WHERE THE REVEREND MISTER BARBEL
IN A PULPIT MADE OF MARBLE
SHOWS HE CAN QUOTATIONS GARBLE.

NOW, ACROSS THE MEAD, THE MINNOW,
SMILING SWEETLY, FRESH AND INNO-
-CENT A MAIDEN AS YOU'D SEE
IN THE WATERS OF THE SEA,
COMES A-TRIPPING,
COMES A-SKIPPING,
WHILE THE SLY OLD TROUT
AND GRAYLING
WATCH HER, LOOKING THROUGH
THE PALING.

interesting for me because it involved a lot of conservation, which was a real enthusiasm of mine, particularly when farm pollution began to be a real problem.'

Unusually for a riverkeeper, Jim worked in an area of the country that is both densely populated and close to London. This caused problems in a multitude of different ways, as he explained.

'Pollution was the really big problem for us because the local sewage works' consent conditions – that's how much sewage they were legally allowed to pump into the river – had been relaxed. There was nothing we could do about it, but at least when things went wrong and we suffered a big pollution we were able to keep the pressure on them for compensation.

'Flow levels were much reduced over the years I worked, too. The local towns took an awful lot of water through abstraction. But my great fear was that one massive pollution was going to come along one day and wipe out all our fish. It was like being on a knife's edge. We were a sort of disaster waiting to happen.

'The other big problem on the Sussex Ouse I suppose was that coarse and game fishermen had to get along side by side and they weren't always able to do it. Don't let anyone tell you they're all brothers of the angle. That's nonsense. They couldn't be more different. I don't know why it was but the game fishermen were nearly always clean and tidy while the coarse fishermen were not so good, in fact some of them were bloody awful. I don't know why they had to chuck their rubbish all over the place.

'Then, of course, with so many new housing developments round and about we always suffered a fair bit of poaching. I spent a lot of time just sitting and waiting to catch them, but we had a good relationship with the police and the local grapevine helped. We knew a lot of the poachers and where they were.'

Jim always made light of these poaching problems, but the potential seriousness of the situation can be judged by the fact that he was once badly injured in a poaching attack:

'Oh yes that was a bit of a do. I'd seen a fellow with a net in the river and a sea trout. I challenged him, I know that sounds a bit threatening but what I mean is I just asked him if he had permission to fish. Next thing I knew I was covered in mud and blood. I had to be taken to hospital and I had nine stitches in my lip. They caught the man who thumped me and he was fined £50 for assault. The thing that got me most about the incident was the surprise. I just didn't expect him to hit me.

'Over the years I was threatened many times, despite the fact that I was always careful when I approached people who weren't supposed to be fishing. I didn't mind so much when it was a youngster fishing where he shouldn't have been – some of the younger ones turn out to be good fishermen in the end.'

Jim always gave the impression of enormous high spirits even when speaking about potentially depressing matters, but after his long years on the river he never lost his sense of the river's ability to enchant all those who became involved with it. He reckoned this had a great deal to do with the river's unique reputation for giant sea trout:

'I think the main reason the society was set up all those years ago was that, even then, they realised the value of the river. The society was actually started by a group of farmers who wanted to preserve the Ouse and its fishing. And in those days the river really was worth preserving. It used to produce some really massive sea trout. The record is held, I believe, by the late John Rench. He landed a sea trout of 16¾lb, but those early fish – for which, unfortunately, we don't have exact records – undoubtedly often weighed over 20lb. The river was always renowned for its big fish. It never produced large numbers. It's odd, but that's what makes it so unique.

'In some ways the river's future was more secure towards the end of my time than it ever had been before, although, after serious floods in 1960, the water authority dredged the river in a very insensitive way. They pulled out far too many trees, threw up great banks and generally altered the character of the river for the worse and, in fact, the fishing suffered. These days I think they would be a bit more careful with their dredgers. The saddest thing I remember wasn't the dredging, it was the time we had a serious outbreak of disease among the fish. I remember walking the banks one day in the early sixties and every few yards I pulled out another 14 or 15lb sea trout. It was terrible, but there was nothing we could do except let the disease take its course. Then, to top it all, we had that other terrible disease, UDN, in the seventies. We found hundreds of fish running into the sidestreams and dying.'

What made Jim so continually surprised by his stretch of the Ouse and the quality of its fishing was the fact that, superficially at least, it looked – and looks – so unprepossessing:

'Oh yes it's a funny old river and when you look at it you'd never think any decent fish would ever bother to come into it, but come they do. Most people who fished for sea trout during my time used a Mepps. The Sussex Ouse is not really a fly river, although a friend of mine – he's the local expert really – had one on a fly. I landed a sea trout of 15lb myself, but that was in 1967 when there were a lot more fish than there are now. Mind you they always seemed to come and go in cycles. We'd have a bad period followed by an upturn and then things got bad again. I would say that in an average year we used get about 150 fish, but they would all have been big.'

The Ouse Angling Preservation Society had some four hundred members in Jim's day, most of whom concentrated on the river's excellent coarse fishing. There were numerous 5lb chub, roach to over 2lb and vast shoals of good-sized bream. Some of

the members came from London and beyond, but most were locals. The Ouse is not a chalkstream, it relies on rainfall for its flow and there was little weed-cutting to be done. 'We never really had to cut the weed in my early days, but with more and more fertiliser getting washed into the river from surrounding farms we had to start. Fertiliser really gets the weed going.'

Apart from worries about weed growth and pollution Jim spent a lot of time worrying about the next oddity he'd find in the river:

'Oh we had some hilarious hunts for all kinds of things,' he says with a grin. 'I remember many years ago our local MP, who was a keen fisherman, mentioned a constituent who kept a crocodile as a pet and when the crocodile grew too big for its tank, the owner put it in the bath. Then, of course, it grew too big for the bath and he put it in the river. We electro-fished to try to catch it – I'm sure the story was true – but we never found it. We've also had terrapins in the river. A mate of mine once caught one on a great big piece of mackerel. Mind you, come to think of it, I wonder why he was fishing with mackerel bait in the first place!'

Jim smiled gleefully at this point and invited me to go down to the river and walk the banks with him. I saw exactly what he meant when he had earlier described the river as unlikely looking. The stretch I walked looked pretty much like a drainage ditch. Jim was being generous when he said the water authority had dredged it insensitively. That was putting it mildly. But in spite of everything, we soon spotted several chub that looked well over 4lb and in an old mill pool Jim pointed out an enormous shoal of big bream sunning themselves. Jim clearly enjoyed talking about his river. Indeed he almost took a fatherly interest in it and he has many stories of strange goings on up and down the banks.

'I know this sounds ridiculous, but one thing we used to get a lot of was safes – you know bank safes. People seemed to make a habit of chucking them into the river. We used to find them under the bridges.

'One of the strangest incidents in my time happened late one night. I was just going home when a chap came up to me and told me he'd been fishing with his wife and they'd seen a ghost. I was a bit sceptical, but he really seemed genuinely frightened. He was absolutely convinced he'd seen something. I thought no more about it, but then I remembered someone else had contacted our local radio station about ghosts down by the river. The chap who'd phoned the radio station said the ghost he'd seen looked like a Roman soldier and I think that was significant because it just happened that the ghost had been spotted at a point on the river where the Romans are known to have had a crossing place. But if the Roman soldier story was true that meant we had two ghosts because the fisherman who'd come up to me said he'd seen a fully dressed woman throw herself into the river from a bridge. He was so convinced we decided to check all the local missing persons lists. He said she'd been wearing a white shawl and a veil and I really think he must have seen something because he never fished here again.

'But perhaps the funniest thing that ever happened to me was when I rescued someone who'd fallen in. I just happened to pass by a couple who were both fishing. They weren't fishing very close together and just as I passed the woman she slipped and fell in. I heard her scream so I ran across to help. I grabbed her to pull her out and the next thing I knew her dress had come right off in my hands.'

Gales of laughter from Jim. Like most riverkeepers he took things as they came. He never had the luxury of an assistant, although there were always one or two part time helpers, but then his job was very much a one-man operation – despite the fact that there was a lot of river to look after.

Jim's day usually started at about eight in the morning and often didn't end till eleven at night.

'A typical day for me started with an early morning walk along the different sections of the river. Then I used to drop in and take a look at our reservoir. I'd check the footpaths, tidy the banks, check regularly for pollution and, of course, keep my eyes peeled for poachers. I also issued water authority licences. I suppose I was a bit like the local bobby on his beat. It was a good life, though, because I got to meet the members and I know many of them very well. Our oldest member was ninety-five and we had several in their eighties, one of whom always insisted on fishing with a fly despite his lack of success. We had several Members of Parliament on the membership list and entertainers like Frankie Vaughan came down to fish now and then.'

Apart from human poachers, Jim also had to put up with the predations of mink and cormorants: 'Those damned cormorants were a nuisance. They used to fly up the valley and take a lot of our fish, particularly if the smolts were running. The mink problem really only started in the sixties when there was a sudden craze for mink farms. There were a lot of escapees and, of course, they played havoc with our fish. There was a local mink hunt which did reduce the numbers a bit.

In spite of being attacked by a poacher, Jim's favourite story was a poaching one. 'The Ouse runs through Lord Callaghan's land and on one occasion we heard that there was some poaching going on down at his place. What started as a small poaching warning ended up as a full-scale security alert. Someone, somewhere, obviously hit the button and suddenly there were hundreds of police everywhere. That poacher must have got the fright of his life when the helicopters came circling round him. I only hope it was the bugger who hit me.'

FISHING
WITH BIGGLES

─────────── ∞∞∞∞ ───────────

George Smith of Grantown-on-Spey enjoyed a reputation as one of the most amusing gillies in Britain. 'A one-hour conversation with George flies by,' said one of his clients. 'Almost painfully funny at times,' said another.

George's reputation had a lot to do with his keen memory and vast fund of extraordinary and delightful anecdotes – many of them verging on the libellous, but all good hearted and very funny. I went to meet him in the cottage just outside Grantown where he was born in 1927. He never moved away from the house that overlooks the river where he spent the whole of his working life. An instantly likeable man, warm, welcoming and generous, he was also a goldmine of information.

Until he retired George had been a gillie on the same stretch of the Spey for nearly fifty years and during that time he met and fished with some of the best-known anglers in Britain, but his strongest and warmest memories were of Captain W. E. Johns, the author of the Biggles books. 'W. E. Johns was a great pal of mine. He was a really super man, well he was until he married his secretary. She was a dreadful woman. He was a really keen fly fisherman, but if we ever had high water he would always stop fishing and so would his guests. They weren't allowed to fish because at high water Captain Johns let all the locals fish. Yes, he was a great man. When the water got right up I used to go round and tell the farmers and their sons to get down to the river and start fishing. Captain Johns would sit on his verandah with his hat tipped back on his head and watch them all fish his water. He loved it. I used to sit with him some-times and he'd often come down to the cottage in the morning to have a cup of tea with my wife and me.

'One of the oddest things about Captain Johns was that all his friends seemed to own white Rolls Royces. I recall Major Waddington always had a white Rolls. He was a great pal of Captain Johns. The captain himself had an enormous Buick in the early fifties and I remember refusing to go and get it once. It was huge and I'd never driven anything like it. Mind you I went to get it eventually – I had to.

'He used to come and take the whole of our stretch of the river every year. I think that in total he came for seven years. He bought a house here too, and long ago we used to shoot duck together. He was one of the finest sportsmen I've ever met and I've been on the river a very long time. Mind you, having said that, I have to say that he was also a mean bugger. He wouldn't give you a penny, although he was incredibly generous with everything else – his fishing and his shooting and so on. He had to be generous with friends like his. The major, one of Captain Johns' friends whom I won't name – was a nice chap but a terri-ble cheat. Really terrible. Maybe it was because he'd started out with no money – he'd won it all on the gambling tables during a cruise it was said. Captain Johns used to say to me when they were both here fishing together: "Go down and see if the major is spinning." And sure enough every time I went down to find him, there he was spinning … and spinning wasn't allowed. I can remember the major's last day on the river. We were on a pool called the Slates. He'd hooked a fish and John Duncan, one of the gillies, had seen him hook it on a prawn, which, like the spinning, wasn't allowed. John shouted to him to get him to shake the fish off, but he wouldn't. In fact he pulled on that rod so hard he broke it. I don't think he could really help himself at moments like that, he just desperately wanted to catch fish. He was greedy for them.

'Captain Johns caught a lot of fish, but he was always happy with just two in a day. And he paid for everyone and everything – all in. To be honest he was also very good to me. After five o'clock every evening he would let me fish and invite anyone I wanted. Mind you, I always put plenty of salmon in the larder for him. I remember once I put nine fish in the larder. He didn't know who'd put them there and he came down the next morning shouting "Who the bloody hell caught those fish?" I think he thought they'd been poached by someone. I told him eventually that I'd caught them under the bridge at Pitchroy the night before and I'd caught them all in one pool. I also told him how I'd caught those fish, but I'm not sure he believed me. I'd used a tuft of hair from the old Alsatian dog I kept then and glued it on to the body of a Black Doctor fly using nail varnish – that did the trick with nine salmon. When I told the Captain that I'd got all the fish on a fly made from the dog he said 'Don't tell those other bastards – they'll pluck your dog for you.'

George chuckled at the memory of his friend. By this time we'd gone from tea to something a little stronger so we raised our glasses to the captain and the major. Over the years George gillied for many celebrities including Lord Denning and the golfer Sandy Lyle:

'Lord Denning was a nice chap. When he arrived he always came straight in to see us here. He usually came in the second week of September with Lord Kimberley, as his guest. Sandy Lyle came down here to fish too. Mind you, he's no bloody good at it at all!'

Roars of laughter from George whose judgements were

always hard edged, but delivered very much tongue in cheek except when he didn't identify an individual by name. If they were left nameless you really could be sure they were beyond the pale. And George had a curious technique for assessing a person's character.

'Names never meant anything to me. I don't judge someone by what they're called or who they are. It's their eyes that matter. I don't give a bugger who it is – I can read them all through their eyes. I'll give you an example. There was one old bugger who used to come up here to fish and I knew straight away he was a bad one. Later on I watched him hook a fish, lose it, and then blame the loss on a great friend of mine. I told him he couldn't blame my friend, but the problem with that fisherman was greed: he was just too greedy for fish. But we'd got the worst weeded out by the time I retired. Only the best came to fish towards the end.' Among the many characters who used to fish with George was a German aristocrat called Friedrich Prinz Zu Hohenlohe-Bartenstein. Until his death the Prince always arrived at the river in a helicopter and with an armed guard.

'Yes, he'd come flying in and then he'd get a car which he'd fill with all sorts of wines. It was always full – always. And his party never seemed to bother to fish much – they just stood and cast. And the bodyguard, who had a revolver, I think, was always going missing anyway. He was so interested in the trout fishing that he used to disappear. They could never find him when they wanted him. The Prince used to bring the Princess with him. She could never fit in her waders because she was so small, but it never used to bother her. She'd just pull them right up almost till they covered her head. When the Prince died my wife and I were invited to the funeral.

'We've had plenty of aristocrats here. One of the funniest was Lord Boothby. He came here on his honeymoon, but he didn't do much fishing – in fact he never left the sheets. That might have had something to do with the fact that his wife was about forty years younger than he was.'

Fishing didn't keep Speyside clear of some of the more momentous political upheavals of the past. After the Profumo scandal John Profumo came up to Speyside in an attempt to escape the world's journalists and to relax with his favourite hobby.

'I didn't really like John Profumo,' says George, 'but I remember him well when he came up just after the big fuss over Christine Keeler. He was out in the river one day and I was just watching when he suddenly panicked. I don't know what had happened – the water was shallow enough – but he was in a bit of a state so although I had no waders on I had to go out to help him.'

George's experiences as a fisherman go right back to the thirties and to his own early days on the river, which were not always happy ones.

'I remember taking home a good fish that I had caught as a wee boy. It was a salmon of about 7lb. I had permission to fish where I caught it, but my father didn't know this. In spite of my explanations he thrashed me and sent the fish back up to Mrs Glenn who owned the fishing. She, of course, immediately sent the fish back down to us in the big car with the chauffeur. The chauffeur explained to my father that I'd been fishing with permission, but my father never apologised for the thrashing he'd given me.'

If George's father's behaviour seemed incomprehensible then so, too, must the many antics that different anglers got up to over the years. One in particular stuck in George's mind.

'Well it was the strangest thing. I was out with a lady who had never fished before, this was many years ago, and she was playing a fish that weighed about 22lb. Everything was going quite well until her husband came along and decided that the only problem was that the rod was bending. He grabbed the end of the rod and tried to straighten out the bend caused by the fish, and he tried to do it while his wife was playing the fish!'

George was no stranger to big fish. In his day he landed salmon to over 30lb on the fly and on one notable day had salmon of 26lb, 28lb and 32½lb all on the fly and in one afternoon. One of his best known regular clients was the Princess of Wales' mother Mrs Shand-Kydd. 'Yes, she used to come up regularly. She's was a marvellous woman, but she never minced her words I can tell you. I was sitting in the back of the car with her one day and we were having a dram when another lady wandered past and stared at her. As she passed Mrs Shand-Kydd said in an audible whisper: "Who the bloody hell are you looking at?"'

George always took a lighthearted view of the many problems faced by the gillie, including the ever-present menace of poaching. But he was always able to deal pretty effectively with persistent offenders.

'We used to get problems with miners coming up in numbers for their holidays, but my big labrador and my Alsatian were well able to keep them on their toes.

'I remember I spotted a poacher's car one day so I went over to it and pulled out the spark-plug leads before going to get help from Captain Johns, who sent for the police. I sent my Alsatian after one of the poachers when I saw him. That was a great dog, she didn't bite him, she just tipped him over when she caught up with him. Once we had him I sent her across the river to deal with the other poacher. I followed in the boat and when I got there she already had him pinned down. Funnily enough that poacher was quite a nice man. He lost his car because I'd messed it up, but he was quite open about the fact that he'd poached the river every Wednesday since the war. He told me that one pool could net him enough salmon to buy a new car. Mind you

he came to a sticky end. He was drowned a few years later trying to swim across the River Dee, which was in flood, to escape
the police.'

Life on the river was clearly a lot of fun for George. Apart
from big fish and good company, George had the pleasure – as
he explained with a grin – of toppling into the river on more
than one occasion. 'Oh, I fell in many times. I remember once
fishing with Captain Johns and talking to him at the same time.
Next minute I was in the river up to my ears. I still don't know
what happened. Captain Johns thought the whole thing was
very funny and he laughed his head off.

'Another time I was just in the process of casting across the
river when one of those bloody fighter jets from Lossiemouth
came screaming over. It came right over my head just as I made
my forward cast and I don't know why, but I followed the cast
straight into the river.'

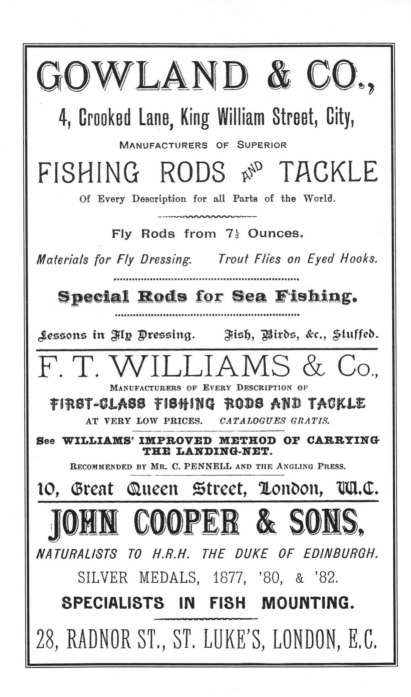

A WONDERFUL
COMPANION

———— ◦◦◦◦◦ ————

Prince Charles once described Bernard Aldrich, river-keeper on the Broadlands Estate in Hampshire for more than thirty years, as 'a wonderful companion on the river'. The Prince went on to praise Bernard's sense of humour, cheerful personality and commitment to, and deep love for, his river. Bernard Aldrich was born in London, in Woolwich, in 1929 and came from a background with no fishing connections. So how did it all start?

'Well I suppose it was luck really,' explained Bernard when I went down to meet him at the Broadlands fishing hut. 'When I left school I served in the Merchant Navy for a while. I left the Navy to get married and became a policeman, but again this was only for a short time. My sister married a Romsey boy and my wife and I used to come down for holidays. I met my predecessor, Walter Geary, during one of these holidays. He'd been keeper on the river for fifty-two years. I got friendly with him and at this time Lord Mountbatten, who owned the estate, was nagging Walter to get a replacement for when he retired. Old Walter used to say to me "I don't know what to do. I don't know anyone who could take over." So one day I said to him "What about me?" We went along after that to see Commander Neill, who was the agent, and I started work. This would have been in 1956. I worked with Walter for five or six years and then he handed the reins to me.

'Long after he'd retired I used to go and get him and bring him down to the river – we were like a big family. Walter knew all those who came to fish and he liked to come down just to be with them and to fish with them.'

Bernard's stretch of the Lower Test was famous for its salmon fishing, but like most of the chalkstream keepers he saw stocks dwindle over the years up to his recent retirement. He was convinced that the river had become dirtier over the years and this pollution together with the pressure of increasing numbers of people also disturbed the wildlife.

'We used to have otters, but as the numbers of people coming down increased they gradually vanished. We disturbed them and they went away. It's very sad. When I first came it was all much wilder. There was no track down to the river. If you wanted to fish you had to walk down or risk driving across a very muddy field.'

For Bernard, work on the river long ago settled into a regular pattern. He started work each day before eight and didn't finish until eight or nine in the evening.

'First thing every morning I went down to our fish farm to clean up and feed the young fish. Then I would wait for the first anglers to arrive. The regulars went straight to the beats where they were booked. If strangers were coming I'd take them down and show them where to fish, and, if necessary, how to fish. Basically I just gave them as much information as I could about the river. Usually it was sons, wives and daughters who came along and needed to be shown how to cast. We had a rota for the fishing and, all told, we had five miles of main river and three miles of trout fishing on the carriers.'

Over the years Bernard taught or assisted a veritable *Who's Who* of famous anglers including Princess Grace of Monaco, Prince Rainier, Admiral Nimitz from the USA and Douglas

Fairbanks Junior. But the anglers he remembers most vividly are Prince Charles and Earl Mountbatten:

'Mountbatten only fished during my early days. He was pretty good at it as I recall, but he didn't really have any great enthusiasm for the sport. Prince Charles, on the other hand, had always been very keen. He was taught to fish by his Scottish gillie and by me. He would have been about five when I first knew him and Mountbatten used to bring him down to the river with Princess Anne.

'I can remember one occasion when Mountbatten asked me to find a salmon for the two children to see. I found one under a bridge where there was usually a fish. The problem with fish in this position was that you had to lower the bait to them from the upstream side of the bridge. Then when you hooked the fish you had to let it tear off downstream unhindered. If two people knew what they were doing, one would hook the fish, let the line fall slack and then drop the rod in the river so that it would drift downstream under the bridge. The angler below the bridge would then pick up the rod. Once fisherman and fish were on the right side of the bridge it was a relatively easy matter to play the fish. Everything went according to plan with the two royal children lying flat on their faces on the bridge, peeping through the bridge planks down into the water where the fish was lying waiting for the bait. It was taken by the fish, but the Earl then forgot to let the line go slack. He held on so tightly that the fish got off. The Prince was the only one who said anything. He just said: "My daddy wouldn't have lost the fish."'

After their wedding Prince Charles and Princess Diana came to Romsey for their honeymoon. As Bernard recalls, this was a time he found more than a little trying.

'Those damned journalists never stopped pestering us the whole time the couple were here. We were quite literally under siege. Reporters arrived twenty-four hours a day. They tried bribing the staff for information – they tried bribing me. I would have quite happily shot a few of them. They really were buggers. My phone used to ring at five in the morning. And they used to ask such stupid questions like "Are they enjoying themselves?" I used to just keep repeating that it was a private visit and it was going to stay private. I even had a chap from the *Melbourne Times* ring me up. Mind you the fact that we said nothing made absolutely no difference. They just made up what they hoped we'd say.'

Bernard had an unusually close relationship with several members of the Royal Family and has nothing but praise for them:

'They always did their utmost to put people at their ease, but of course we all get tongue-tied, which is the last thing they want. We hold them in awe, but I genuinely believe that they don't see themselves as anything out of the ordinary. Whether it's Prince Charles or the Queen Mother – who also fished here – they are always quite happy to follow your suggestions about where and how to fish. If I used to say try there or over there they would always do it.'

In his time at Broadlands, Bernard saw many changes and not just in terms of the increasing sophistication of tackle and techniques. He also charted the immense social changes that took-place during his thirty-five years on the river. In a way the river was a microcosm of the erosion, in the wider world, of restricting social barriers.

'The changes were perhaps most obvious in terms of dress. People used to come down dressed specifically to fish. They all wore tweeds and I wore a tweed suit and a hat and tie bought specially for me by the estate. I think all that formality began to disappear as younger, more affluent people began to come down to fish. In the old days I wouldn't have dreamed of calling anyone by their Christian name. I was always expected to call everyone "Sir". Towards the end I was on first name terms with about 95 per cent of those who fish at Broadlands, but I still remember that old tweed suit. I used to get a new one every year, complete with plus-fours.'

In those early days Bernard was also expected to take great care of each angler's tackle – down to the last detail. 'There was no nylon when I first came. It was just starting to come in, but it was viewed with great suspicion. Everyone still used catgut. It came in short lengths – each piece was about 1ft long – and it had to be knotted together to make a decent length. It was thick stuff too and very stiff, so you had to damp each piece overnight.

'We had what were called cast dampers – they were like small felt pads. You packed about six casts in these to keep them nice and supple. At lunchtime we'd put the casts into the river to keep them from stiffening. The great thing about gut was that it turned over beautifully when you cast. Ordinary nylon just doesn't turn over properly, that's why people started to use braided nylon for their casts.

'I can remember the old greenheart rods: the Grant Vibration and the Castle Connel. Greenheart had a very slow action and it weighed a ton. Greenheart rods were also spliced. A lot of people today just don't realise how different things were then. The rods had no ferrules – the sections were just lashed together with leather thongs – that was literally all that kept them together. They vanished long before I retired but I thought their demise was sad as they were beautifully made things. Apart from their weight the great problem with greenheart rods was that they dried out badly and one day you'd be fishing and they'd literally explode in a cloud of dust – usually when you were into a good fish.

'When I first came here I knew every angler's rod and its peculiarities. I'd take them out of the fishing hut ready for whoever I knew was coming to fish. We had a lot to do for each angler then. We'd rub goose fat into the silk line, soak their casts in the river, run their silk lines off the reels and wind them onto wooden line-driers. These were like big wooden reels. At the end of each season each line would be dressed with French chalk to get it through the winter without rotting.

'Although a lot of hard work went out of the riverkeeper's job because of the improvements in fishing tackle, we didn't feel we were a lot better off because there always seemed to be more to do on the river, with bank maintenance, repairing the fishing huts and the bridges. We also had a coarse-fishing lake to look after and although there were three of us, in the very early days there were four, and that was in the days before we had the fish farm and the lake. Keeping the banks in order was always been a sod of a job, but it had to be done.'

The trout fishing at Broadlands was always good, but towards the end of his time on the river, Bernard had to stock the river with fish bred on the estate. The salmon situation was more worrying.

'There's no doubt that the salmon fishing just wasn't as good at the end of my time as it had been twenty years earlier. We caught sixty fish in 1988. That's not a large number, but it was a slight improvement on the previous year which was our worst ever. In that year we caught just thirty-nine fish. The problem, of course, is that we had no control over the high-seas netting industry.'

But if the anglers failed to find as many salmon in the river as they would have liked, they certainly found some strange items over the years. Bernard again:

'We found a mass of strange wooden piles in the river years

ago. They were obviously very old and they certainly weren't part of any river maintenance work that had ever been carried out. We contacted someone from the Mary Rose Trust who came and took away some samples of the wood, but we never heard another word about it. Other odd things have turned up in the river from time to time, terrapins, for example. I was gutting a fish one day when what looked like a small turtle suddenly swam up out of the depths of the river and grabbed some of the bits and pieces floating away from the fish. I managed to catch that terrapin and we put it in his lordship's fountain where it remains to this day.'

The present owner of Broadlands is Lord Romsey, who doesn't fish. Lady Romsey was once very keen and she was taught by Bernard.

Other curious items found in the river over the years include an unexploded 16in shell. This was spotted lying in clear water in the middle of the river and it caused something of a panic. As it turned out the shell wasn't quite what it seemed.

'Yes, we were very worried about that shell so we brought the military in to defuse it or blow it up carefully or whatever. When they got here the whole thing turned into a bit of an embarrassment because the shell was actually just a piece of wood. Mind you, even the bomb disposal people were astonished at how much it looked like a real shell. In fact they were so impressed that they took it away for their museum. It was sheer chance that the wood had been weathered to look like a bomb.'

Bernard still laughs at the memory of the phoney shell and he has many other happy memories from his early days at Broadlands, particularly from the time when he worked with Walter Geary:

'Oh, yes, Walt was a bit of a joker. I remember one very funny trick he pulled on a group of Americans. We used to catch massive, well-mended kelts in the river in February and one day Walter was just in the process of returning a particularly fresh-looking kelt – it was so clean and silver looking that it really did look like a fresh fish. Anyway, a group of Americans nearby asked why he was putting back such a big fish so Walter told them, with a completely straight face, that it was too small to keep. Their mouths dropped open when they heard that, but Walt never let on. They must have gone away thinking that our takeable fish were absolutely gigantic.'

The record for salmon on the Broadlands fishery is recorded in the estate ledgers which detail every fish caught since the 1880s. It weighed 43lb and was caught in 1883. Since that time other massive fish have been hooked – and lost.

'I remember one almighty fish we hooked down at Webb's Pool. It went tearing round for about half an hour and then charged under the bridge. There was nothing we could do to stop it. We were just passing the rod under the bridge when the line caught on part of the stonework and parted. The most extraordinary thing about that fish was that three days later I found the end of the broken line in the river, tied it to the end of the line on my rod and played the same fish for another twenty minutes before it finally escaped for good. But I can tell you that really was a massive fish.'

The temptations of giant fish mean that Broadlands was also subject to serious poaching. In one incident when Bernard tried to stop a car-load of poachers escaping he was nearly run over:

'I crept down at night and spotted a group of poachers so we phoned the police, but while waiting for the police to arrive I heard a car coming up from the river. I stepped into the road and flashed my torch at the oncoming car thinking it was the police, but the driver accelerated and missed me by inches. In the old days the poachers down here worked alone and they were pretty harmless, but those days had gone by the time I retired. The modern poacher doesn't just take one fish, he takes as many as he can get away with and is quite willing to attack you in the process. I was lucky I suppose – luckier anyway than our gamekeeper. He was shot in the face by poachers and was lucky to survive.'

Despite retirement Bernard Aldrich still lives on the Broadlands estate and with his dogs and regular visits to the river he says he is busier than ever.

RIVERKEEPING'S GREATEST DYNASTY

꘎꘎꘎꘎꘎

Mick Lunn belongs to what was probably the most famous riverkeeping dynasty in the world. He was the third generation of Lunns to have worked on the Houghton water on the Test below Stockbridge in Hampshire. Mick's grandfather William started on the river in 1886. William's father had drowned when his ship sank on the way to America and William was brought up by his stepfather. When I interviewed Mick he still remembered William.

'Oh yes, he was a real character was William. He had a difficult life as a boy because his stepfather was a very hard man. William did all sorts of different jobs as a young man and he ended up, before he came down to Houghton, as a bank messenger in Princes Street in London. I suppose that's how it all started because the president of the bank was a keen fisherman and a member of the Houghton Club. He brought my grandfather down to the river and discovered that he had a real aptitude for the work. Soon after that William was offered the job of riverkeeper and he eventually made a name for himself as one of the finest natural historians of the chalkstreams. My grandfather also invented one of the most famous trout flies still in use: Lunn's Particular. He also tied the first Houghton Ruby. I think the Particular was invented around about 1900.' Like his father and grandfather before him Mick, who was born in 1927, formerly looked after the stretch of the Test owned and run by what is generally considered the most exclusive – and some would say secretive – fishing club in the world. The Houghton Fishing Club may also be the oldest formally organised fishing club in the world, as Mick explained when I met him at Stockbridge.

'The club actually started life in the little village of Houghton where, incidentally, I was born. The club was started in 1822 by Canon Beadon and Edward Barnard. They were fishing friends and one day they happened to walk into a pub in Houghton where they discovered somehow or other that the fishing lease was up for sale on the river nearby. This was the lease on the lower part of the 15 miles owned by the club. After a few years they lost the lease on that water – I believe they lost it for a year – but by then they'd managed to lease the fishing on the upper

FLIES.—No. 4.

Three artificial Salmon Flies.
1. Jay Fly for Salmon.
2. Peacock Fly for Salmon.
4. Bee, a natural Bait for a Chub.
5. Devil, an artificial Bait for Trout.
6. A natural May Fly, or Green Drake

water. Eventually the chap who owned all the fishing sold the freehold to the club.'

Mick was speaking as we walked along the beautifully kept banks of the river where he spent all his working life. Unlike most riverkeepers and gillies whose main problems have to do with poaching and pollution, Mick seems to have suffered most from the attention of journalists. 'Well, I was always being contacted by journalists from all over the world and some of them were pretty persistent. I didn't mind speaking to them, but I didn't like to say too much about how rich – or otherwise – the Houghton Club members were. I didn't mind talking about the river and the fishing, but a lot of journalists were not really interested in the fishing. They always seemed to be after the social-class aspect of the whole thing. I always told them they were lucky I was speaking to them at all: my father and grandfather both had a strict rule that they would never speak to journalists and they never did.'

Rather than risk being tipped into the river I steered clear of too many questions about the members, but from the few remarks Mick did make it seems that they are quite a remarkable bunch. For a start there are only twenty-four of them and new members may join only when one of the existing members dies. No members of the Royal Family are said to be members, but Mick confided to me that over the years one or two royals had come down to fish the Houghton water. There was always a long waiting list for membership; apart from anything else, the club had – and still has – some of the finest dry-fly fishing in the world. The 15 miles owned by the club covers both banks and although it is all kept for just twenty-four members, Mick didn't think this made it exclusive.

'The worst thing for good dry-fly fishing is too much pressure on the water. If there were too many people on the river then the quality of the fishing would inevitably have declined. Although we had a stock of wild fish we still had to put extra trout into the river each year. Some of the fish we stocked were of takeable size when they went in, others were just fingerlings. We put brown trout in mostly but with a few rainbows, because they're such eager risers.'

Mick is in a unique position among riverkeepers because his memories of the river and how it was fished long ago include a great deal of material handed down from the middle of the last century. Mick described for me the fly-fishing technique of those early days.

'In the middle of the last century, fly fishing as we know it today, simply didn't exist. It was all what I suppose we would call "blow fishing". They impaled a live insect on a hook and then let it blow out over the water. There was none of the kind of casting you get today. It was only towards the end of the century, after my grandfather came here, that the "whipping rod" came into use with enough spring in it to propel a fly out over the water. Before fishing could be carried out effectively with the artificial fly, the fishermen used to come for just two short periods each year: the hatching of the grannom and then the mayfly. That was a total fishing time of only six weeks. The rest of the time the river had hardly any fishing pressure at all, but once they discovered that the artificial fly could work really well – in the 1890s – everyone fished much more.

'From those early days of greenheart rods and then cane, we've had a revolution in tackle, of course, and hardly anyone used cane towards the end of my time on the river. I have to add, too, that I never missed the old tackle. New rods are so light and there's no messing about with greased silk lines. Mind you a number of our members were still using silk lines in the early sixties, but then fishermen are very conservative and they change their ways slowly. I don't know why else they kept using those old silk lines – they were a lot more work because you had to grease them at the start of every day and then dry them off carefully when you'd finished fishing.'

William Lunn retired in 1931 and died a few years later when Mick was about twelve. Already by that time Mick's father, Alfred, had worked for a number of years on the river as a kind of apprentice. And this was the same system Alfred was eventually to adopt with Mick. He worked alongside Alfred for more than twenty years, until 1962 when he finally took over as headkeeper.

'My grandfather lived until he was in his eighties and when my father died he was seventy-three. He had about eight years of retirement and he fished all the time, but that's the thing about being a riverkeeper. It was never really a job at all – it was a way of life. There were no regular hours and you didn't end up making a fortune, but I never thought of doing anything else. I also think that fishing and longevity go together. They certainly go together if the ages of the Houghton Club members are anything to go by. Our oldest member was well into his eighties when I was still on the river and he had been fishing here for over forty years.' I knew I was sailing back into dangerous waters, but I had to ask how new people are recruited if and when a vacancy arises:

'Well, when a member died the name of a possible new member was put forward and there was a vote. It was as simple as that: if the members vote yes the new man can join. Being a member is an expensive business too, but it's worth it because the fishing is superb.'

Like many southern chalkstream keepers, Mick regretted the passing of the days of the watermeadows because they did so much to improve the quality of the water.

'Flooding the fields used to clear the sediment from the water and leave it on the land. That did the land a lot of good as well as the water. The war really put a stop to all that. More and more land went under the plough and then the chemicals came and the farmers ploughed right up to the river's edge to squeeze every last penny out of their ground. So with all these changes the water quality was bound to be poorer. There's no question about that.

'When I was a boy the land all about was watermeadows and as a result the river ran as clear as tapwater. But that kind of agriculture was labour intensive and therefore expensive. It never returned when the war ended. Mind you the water was still good in my early days on the river. My barometer for water quality is the fly life – and the fly life here was tremendous. After a series of mild winters I remember we started getting the mayfly a full week earlier than usual and in the late 1980s, as a result, we had some superb seasons. But things were very bad for the mayfly between 1955 and 1975 – over that long period we virtually had no mayfly at all. It takes only a few bad egg-laying seasons – when the wind's constantly in the north and it rains heavily – to put paid to your mayfly. In those conditions the females just won't lay their eggs. Wherever there is an avenue of trees along the river you get a sanctuary area for mayfly. These areas don't tend to lose their stocks simply because the trees protect the insects from the worst of the weather and they then move from these sanctuary areas to repopulate the rest of the river.' Mick's water never had the pressure of fishing that many of his colleagues up and down the river had to cope with, but with weed-cutting and bank maintenance he worked long hours right up to his retirement. The fishermen themselves, he explained, usually arrived at about eleven in the morning:

'We kept a list of which beats were being fished by whom. There were fourteen beats and if you were a member you would just put yourself down for a particular beat and then off you went. It was as simple as that. Beats did change, however, between the morning and the evening sessions.

'I used to go down with the fishermen occasionally. This usually happened if they brought a guest who needed some tuition. Most of my work centred on looking after the trout, though. Everything here was done to nurture the trout, but we were never interested in big individual fish. Fish of 2 or 3lb are much more free rising than fish of, say, 10 or 12lb. You'll never see a fish that big unless there's a really heavy hatch of mayfly.

'Mind you in the old days when the pressure of fishing was that much less, wild trout to about 11lb were caught and we still got a few salmon, though fewer and fewer as the years went by. They were normally caught later in the year when the water cleared. I've even seen them caught on a dry fly. We used to get two or three each year.'

With five keepers looking after the Houghton water it should have been safe from the attentions of poachers but even this didn't seem to deter them, as Mick explained: 'Poaching was always a big problem. And the poachers seemed to come from all over the place, usually in twos and threes. They drove the riverkeepers up the wall in the summer and then the gamekeepers in the winter. We usually caught them because we carried out early morning car-spotting patrols. Luckily, fishing being what it is, even the poachers got so absorbed in what they were doing that we were often able to catch them red handed.'

And every last fish mattered in the Houghton Club. Mick again: 'The senior member always wrote up the records in the club headquarters: a room at the Grosvenor Hotel in Stockbridge High Street. In fact club records go right back to

1822 and they include details of individual fish weights, weather conditions at the time each fish was captured and the fly on which they were caught.'

In his quiet way Mick clearly relished the time he spent on the river, but one thing saddened him: he was the last of the line. When he retired the Lunn connection with the Houghton water came to an end after more than a century.

RENDERING THE STREAMS FIT

———————— ◦◦◦◦◦ ————————

T he Piscatorial Society is one of the oldest fishing clubs in the world. Its first meeting was held at the Granby Tavern in London's South Audley Street in 1836. The society was set up, in the words of one of the founders, 'to promote and encourage fair angling and to stimulate harmonious social conversation.'

In those early days the society had fishing on streams and rivers in and around what is now Greater London. But as the suburbs grew and pollution spread, rivers like the Colne, which once produced wild trout to 7lb, began to decline and the society was forced west down into Hampshire and Wiltshire where the crystal chalkstreams provided the kind of fishing the society's members had always cherished.

The records of the society go right back to the earliest days and they provide a fascinating insight into the lives of long-dead members, many of whom achieved fame in the world of angling. Among the best known former members are angling writers like H. T. Sheringham, Alfred Jardine and Frank Buckland.

The club owns some 6½ miles of the Wylye, 1 mile of the Itchen, and 3 miles of leased water on the Avon. For many years the Avon water was looked after by ex-Navy man Tom Ellis. Tom, who was born in 1936, started fishing as a boy in the Midlands and his own fishing career, from coarse fishing in his early days to trout and salmon later on, mirrored that of the society for which he worked. A gentle, kindly looking man, Tom explained all this when I went down to meet him in the village of Lower Woodford.

'Yes, the Piscatorial Society started as a coarse-fishing society, though it's probably fair to say that they didn't make the hard and fast distinctions we now make between the different kinds of fishing. That's why if you look in the early records you'll see that each angler will list the weights of all the different fish he might catch in a day and they must have been very keen on catching pike, for instance, because the arms of the Piscatorial Society chair are carved in the shape of a pike.'

Before moving to the Piscatorial Society's stretch of the Avon Tom worked part time on the River Meon, also in Hampshire:

'The Meon was a lovely little river. I was keeper there for the Portsmouth Flyfishers Association, but the river suffered very badly from abstraction over the years. In fact it's virtually dried up now. I worked on the Meon part time while I was still in the Navy, but when I came out in the early 1960s, I knew I wanted to work as a riverkeeper. I was helped by Alex Behrendt who ran the Two Lakes Stillwater Fishery. He put a word in for me when the job at the Piscatorial Society turned up and that did the trick.

People used to come down in the summer and say to me "You've got a lovely job," but what they forgot is that, in a way, being a riverkeeper is the worst possible job for someone like me who really loves fishing. The fact is that I was always so busy on the river I hardly ever had time to fish myself.

'Like the society I started as a coarse fisherman and then took up trout fishing later. I used to fish Eyebrook Reservoir and Ravensthorpe in the Midlands. Once I became keeper I did continue to fish, but only occasionally and usually for pike and grayling.'

During his long years on the river Tom caught grayling to nearly 3lb and once, while fishing the River Eye in the Midlands, he landed several roach, each weighing more than 2lb – for a coarse fisherman a 2lb roach is usually considered the fish of a lifetime.

But professionally Tom was always more concerned with the welfare of his stocks of trout and, of almost equal importance, his fly life: 'If the river was in good order and you had good fly life then you always knew there was little to worry about. As long as the fly life was prolific we never really bothered much about the fact that we couldn't remove all the coarse fish.'

Somehow that seems rather fitting on a water leased by a club that once paid tribute to the sporting qualities of a range of different fish species. A bigger threat to the trout came, however, from pollution and abstraction. Ironically these were the same problems that pushed the society west more than a century ago. Tom again:

'Two-thirds of our water came from green sandstone and about one third from pure chalk; after the heavy rains of winter the river was usually high and coloured early in the spring. As the levels fell and the weed started to grow vigorously, the particles that make the water look cloudy were filtered out: this is why we didn't start fishing until 1 May. The river was just too cloudy until then. Mind you, some people say it is never now as clear at any time of year as once it was. I think this is because in the old days all the land in this area was put down to grass for the sheep. Modern arable farming caused a terrible wash off of all sorts of chemicals into the river and this, in turn, caused discolouration.

'Apart from farming pollution, there were always problems with abstraction. They took the water from the source of the river not from near the end because that way they didn't have to pay to clean it and although the water authority officials used to tell us that the flow rates were just as they were twenty years ago I was never convinced.

'The problem with abstraction was only one of our troubles. We had an equally serious problem with bank erosion. This was caused by cattle coming to drink. Gradually they'd broken down the banks. The soil was then washed away by flood water and the river gradually widened. With the same amount of water flowing through a wider river you inevitably get a slower current. This happened for many years and it was the main reason why we spent so much time repairing the banks. We drove in wooden piles wherever there had been serious erosion and then backfilled with tons of chalk. When the weeds and plants started to grow the whole thing soon looked natural and it really did help to reduce the width of the river and thereby increase the pace of the water. What this meant, in the long run, was better fishing. It always reminded me of something one of our more famous past members once said about the whole aim of the Piscatorial Society. It was F. M. Halford in 1902. He said: "If dry-fly fishing is to flourish in the future, some class of those affected by it must devote both time and cash to rendering the streams fit for the sport and keeping them up to the mark in that respect."'

Tom's stretch of the Avon included an area where the meadows were still flooded each year, but the area covered was small and the practice continued, according to Tom, simply for historical interest. But he pointed out, with a chuckle, that the flooding system does have its benefits: 'It most certainly does. In that terrible drought of 1976 for example, the watermeadows were the only part of this area with any decent grass. The watermeadows were positively lush.'

Like all the Test and Avon keepers Tom used to cut weed several times a year. 'The days when cutting was permitted were called free days. Our dates for cutting were 3–12 May, 19 June to 6 July, 23 July to 1 August and then 4–8 September. If we wanted to cut at any other time we had to lift all the weed out, but during the free days everyone on the Upper Avon would cut and all the weed was caught down at Salisbury on a boom. We had a boat for cutting weed in the deeper areas, but I always enjoyed doing it by hand, I always thought it was more accurate.'

Among all the other difficulties with which a riverkeeper has to contend, the problem of pollution is never far away, but Tom confessed that he had been lucky. 'The river did change as a result of pollution, but we were looking at a general increase in pollution, not sudden massive illegal pollution. At one time cleaning fluids and small amounts of sewage from houses and farms were no real problem because that was all there was. But with reduced flows and vast amounts of farm pesticides the river just couldn't be as good as it once was. It all had a cumulative effect and the water flow just couldn't cope with it. Luckily, though, we didn't have any trout farms above us – whatever anyone says, trout farms are bad polluters.

'Amesbury Sewage Farm released a lot of effluent into the river once and it killed all our weed, but the water authority was quick to act and pump oxygen into the water – if it's done quickly enough that can save your fish. We didn't lose many fish on that occasion but our fly life was badly affected. And, of course, any compensation is never enough. The fish we were able to restock with couldn't compensate for the ones we'd lost, many of which would have been wild stock. I have to say too that I think the farmers were always let off very lightly. They used to get away with murder because the fines were derisory when they were found guilty of polluting a river.'

Tom's sadness about the state of the river and the effects of the pollution may make him sound rather a glum man. But like most gillies and riverkeepers he was, in fact, remarkably optimistic in spite of everything and he positively glowed when he talked about the plans he had for the river and his efforts to improve the fishing:

'We really wanted the fish population to be self-sustaining, although we knew it would be very difficult. We close the season here on 30 September because the hen fish are well developed with eggs by then. This is our future stock so we took great care of it. We encouraged spawning by raking the gravel where we knew they would breed. Wild-bred stocks of trout were always improving here but we still had to stock with yearling trout in the autumn – say fish of 6 to 9in. We used to put about 1,500 in and then a few extra during the mayfly time because our mayfly hatch was really excellent.

'Grayling are good indicators of the state of the water so we were quite happy to have some in the river, together with a few coarse fish, particularly roach and dace. One keeper here found a 3lb roach dead on the bank. Our biggest ever trout weighed 4lb 6oz, but we never really worried about big fish. There were a few rainbow trout in the river, but these were escapees from trout farms. We only ever stocked with brown trout.

'I used to see a lot of small fish in the river that I knew were wild. They were easily scared and had dark olive-coloured backs and a distinct hump. In terms of fish size a good indication of the way things changed over the years is the fact that one of the best known of all riverkeepers, Frank Sawyer, used to say that his wild trout averaged 1½lb. In my day our very best wild fish would only weigh 1¾lb.

'We also had a catch and release policy here and we tried to encourage people to use barbless hooks. I know there are a lot of arguments against catch and release, but I'm sure it works where you've got running water. On stillwaters I know that rainbows are sometimes found dead a couple of days after being caught and released, but browns don't seem to suffer in the same way. When they're put back carefully there is a very high survival rate. Another problem with catch and release – or maybe it's an advantage – is that the fish are much harder to catch next time.'

Tom laughed and offered to take me to see the society's fishing hut and the river itself. The fishing hut is a remarkable repository of rare items collected over the years by members of the Piscatorial Society. It is all housed in a small room above the electricity generator that first brought power to the villages round about. Long since fallen into disuse, the power house now provides a quiet sanctuary near the river for anglers in need of lunch, a rest or a quiet hour with a book.

The hut contains a superb library of fishing books including some rare Victorian volumes. There are beautifully cased specimen fish, some caught by members more than a century ago, paintings, etchings and, most important for the tired fisherman, comfortable chairs. The preserved specimens, which include pike, tench and two magnificent barbel, bear witness to the wide early interests of the society. Tom showed me the society records dating back to the middle of the last century. Each entry includes detailed information about the species of fish caught, bait used and even the state of the weather. Perhaps the most

remarkable item in the hut is the beautifully carved chair with its pike shaped arms and intricately designed back, which includes fishing scenes and a superbly detailed creel.

When we left the hut Tom took me down to see the river, which meanders in typical chalkstream fashion through lush countryside. He showed me the work he and his fellow keepers had done to repair the damage to the banks caused by erosion and he demonstrated his sharp fish-spotting eye by pointing out ten fish for every one I managed to see. Tom also has some marvellous tales about the somewhat eccentric people the river occasionally used to attract.

'At Lake we were only about 1 mile from Stonehenge and I remember during the middle seventies we always had a few problems during the summer solstice. As I went down to the river one year I heard a lot of shouting and hollering. I couldn't think what it was all about and then I turned a bend in the river and I couldn't believe my eyes: there were about seventy people swimming completely naked. I asked them what they thought they were doing. A bit of a silly question I know, but it was the first thing that came into my head. They just said "We're bathing and this is God's country." I said this is a trout river and trout don't like polluted water. To be fair to them they got out straight away and just wandered off.

'Every year one or two of them – I suppose you'd call them hippies would wander down to the river and they were always completely naked, sometimes they'd even walk naked along the main road. I don't think the local people would have got away with it. But apart from the hippies, and an inexplicable number of large trays of onions that used to come floating down and get stuck in our hatches, the only other problem we ever had was a car that was found one day right in the middle of the river. It must have been pushed down the steep hill from the road and stayed afloat long enough to drift out into the middle. I didn't think much about it until the police asked me to wade out and see if there was a body in it. Luckily, there wasn't.'

Poaching was never a big problem on the river because, as Tom explained, the society's water is near the road and 'any poachers would have had a hard job even to get a few fish here – besides, we had an excellent farm-watch system.'

The Piscatorial Society had about one hundred members and there was always a long waiting list. Potential members were also closely vetted simply to ensure that they did not spoil the fishing for the other members. 'We had quite a variety of different members,' explained Tom. 'We had Admirals of the Fleet, Air Vice-Marshalls, businessmen and actors. Sir Michael Hordern was a life member and he used to fish here regularly with his brother.'

FIFTY YEARS A GILLIE

—————— ⚬⚬⚬⚬⚬ ——————

William Fraser was born in 1913. He was a full-time gillie for nearly fifty years and most of that time was spent in the wilds of Inverness on the River Beauly and its tributaries. According to the tradition of the Highlands, William owed allegiance, as a Fraser, to the head of the Fraser clan, Lord Lovatt. For William this tradition was a practical part of everyday life because Lord Lovatt was also his employer.

'I grew up with the old laird. We were boys together in Strathfarrar. The river, his river, was at my door and in those days there was no employment in this area other than a job that had something to do with fishing or shooting. So all the young men started either as gillies or keepers. I was head stalker for Lord Lovatt for eighteen years, but I'd worked as an assistant for years before that. As headkeeper you might work for one day on the hill after the deer and then the following day you would be on the river.'

Long after he had retired William still took out fishermen who ask for him specially. And after more than fifty years on the river he was still, inevitably, much in demand. A compact, quietly spoken man, he always managed to look much younger than his years and he had the dour good humour for which the Highland gillie is famous. He was also fond of a wee dram and as we talked about days long ago on the Beauly and its tributaries, we settled ourselves round the fire with a glass each of whisky. William's connections with the Highland rivers go back a long way, as he explained:

'My father started on Lord Lovatt's estate in 1902 and my grandfather, who was a shepherd, actually drowned in the River Glass, a tributary of the Beauly. My two brothers, who both died in the war, were also stalkers.

'There were fifty-six keepers on the Lovatt Estate when my father started work as a gillie and they all wore exactly the same tweed suits. They were all made in the Lovatt tweed, which is very distinctive. In fact in those days each estate had its own tweed; the individual tweeds were designed to suit the particular ground on which you would be working. In a sense they were designed, I suppose, to give you the best camouflage. My suits were made by Campbell's of Beauly and they had to be worn at all times.

'When I started work I was actually employed only during the fishing and stalking seasons. It was the same for everyone; when the fishing and stalking stopped you were just out of work. I used to scrape by with the odd bit of work repairing the banks, but it was only when I became headkeeper that I had work right through the year.

'As an ordinary keeper or gillie you would be lucky to get work when there was no fishing or shooting, helping gather in the sheep and clipping them, but that was in the days when almost all the Beauly and its tributaries were owned by the Lovatts.

'I suppose I really started work on the river when I was twelve, but I left for fifteen year's service with the Lovatt Scouts from 1931 and I worked for the hydro-electric board for some years. Mind you that was still river work – I used to operate the fish lifts on the Beauly. I also worked on the Spey for a time, during its heyday between 1953 and 1964. During those years it was nothing to get eighteen or twenty fish in a day to one rod.

'As a boy I was expected to row a boat all day for the guests. I started on the Farrar, a tributary of the Beauly. In those days the whole attitude to fishing was completely different from what it is today. People would rent the fishing and then invite their guests up just for the fun of it. There was no thought of making money out of the fish you caught. In fact, in those days the idea of making money out of it was frowned on.

'We caught a lot of fish in the twenties and thirties, perhaps surprisingly in view of the tackle we used: great heavy wooden reels with a silk line like a rope, massive flies, much bigger than would be used today, and thick white gut. I remember Lord Lovatt caught fifty-six salmon from one pool on that sort of tackle. That was the present Lord Lovatt's grandfather. He was using a massive 18ft rod as I recall. Those early rods were white-wood, greenheart or cane.'

Like most gillies, William was philosophical about the changes that took place among the fishermen during his career. When he'd first started work on the river the fishermen and women were mostly from the South of England 'mostly dukes and lords and ladies,' but towards the end of his time they tended to come from much further afield. 'Yes, they started to come from abroad, particularly from Austria and Germany.' He accepted these changes with equanimity, but he was never happy about changes to the stocks of salmon:

'My strongest memories from early days are of the sheer numbers of fish in the river – I don't think it would be going too far to say that when I started you would often find more fish in one pool than you would find in the whole river today. The problem was the nets all along the coast and even when they were legal netters you have to remember that they only ever took from the river; unlike the rod and line fishermen they never put anything back. The anglers stocked their rivers, protected the reeds where the fish spawned and always put the kelts back. Lots of estates knew that their stocked fish were being taken by the nets so they began to say to themselves, "why should we bother?"

'I think the rivers of the Western Isles were the only ones really worth fishing by the time I retired. On most of our rivers the great days are gone. The fish just don't get the chance to grow big; most are caught at three or four years old and they're just grilse.

'Poaching was also a terrible problem. One man can't do anything about it because it was never just one or two poachers – they came up here by the coachload. They thought it was a sort of free for all. Worse still they often used light tackle and ended up leaving fish with hooks and line trailing from their mouths.'

William assisted and taught hundreds of different people over the years, both fishermen and shooters.

'Well, during my time I've accompanied some very famous people to the river. I remember meeting Prince Charles and watching him fish. This was when my regiment was based at Balmoral. And much earlier I can remember going out shooting with King George VI, Lord Lovatt and Lord Lucas. I had to sort out the different parties for the grouse butts. King George VI always got the most birds, largely because the head keeper would always shout "That's His Majesty's bird" whenever a grouse came anywhere near the King even if it wasn't, strictly speaking, his bird at all.

'The present Queen was only sixteen then, but I remember her well and I can remember Margaret too. She was a real madam even then! George VI was also a very keen fisherman and he was pretty good at it too.' `William laughed quietly and raised his glass to the memory of these notables.

'I'm not really thinking about them. I'm just remembering that in spite of all the time the lords and ladies spent fishing the Beauly, the biggest ever salmon from the river was caught by

Lord Lovatt's butler. I can remember it well. The butler was called Mr Vickers and he worked up at Beaufort Castle. This was in the days when the gentlemen still retired after dinner to smoke. They'd got to this stage in the proceedings when Lord Lovatt rang for the butler and discovered he'd gone down to the river. He found out later that the butler had spent four and a half hours playing a salmon just 4oz under 50lb. That was a very big fish indeed, particularly when you think that round about 20lb is usually the biggest we get this far up the river. In the old days the Kilmorack Falls stopped the big fish getting up. It's been dammed since and they even put lifts in for the fish, but it never persuaded the big ones to come up. Sea trout never used to get through the falls either, and they still don't.

'I can remember an angler losing an almighty fish. It was a Mr Smith I think and he played the fish for nearly five hours before it was lost. The gillie who was out that day said it was the biggest fish he had ever seen – perhaps it would have beaten the record.

'Most of the gillie's work here involved helping the fisherman get the most from his or her day on the river. We simply went down to the river with whoever was fishing and advised them on how best to fish under the circumstances. Some knew the river well and needed less help, but you still showed them the lies in each pool and told them which fly to use, what size the fly should be and so on. Most importantly when they hooked a fish you had to help them land it. At one time we gaffed all the fish, but latterly everyone used nets. It's less cruel. Sometimes an angler would get tired or fed up and give you the rod, but if you ever hooked a fish you always gave the rod straight back.

'When a lady was fishing you always waded out and stayed with her. On a big river you'd have a boat and let it down each pool with a rope. We used a very flat-bottomed boat to reduce the pull of the water and the gillie dropped anchor at the head of the pool and then gradually let the anchor rope slip through his fingers as the fisherman worked his way down.

'It was the appearance of the fishermen and women that changed most over the years I think. Fishing technique stayed just the same – at the end of my time I still taught people exactly the things my own father had taught me – but dresswise things have changed enormously. In the 1930s all the women dressed in such a way that they looked old at forty. Now they all look great at eighty. Mind you having said all that, I have to admit that the same was never really true of the men. Some never changed at all – they still wore their tweed suits just as they always had!

'In my time I've seen some very good fishermen and women. I remember a Miss Toynbee from Kent. She used to come up to fish when I was a boy and she always waded into the river to gaff her own fish. That was very unusual in those days. Mind you, the good, skilled fisherman doesn't always catch the most fish; often with salmon fishing it's the novice who gets the fish.

'Some of my clients had been with me for over forty years and I've taught four generations of the same family – the Burns from Dundee – to fish. Among the men one of the best fishermen I can remember was Lord Encomb. He was really excellent although I have to admit that in those days there were so many fish in the river that almost anyone could catch them.

'Some fishermen don't worry too much about actually catching fish. I remember a doctor I used to take out trout fishing on the loch. Once we went out in a dead calm and I told him it was probably hopeless, but he just said, "I couldn't care less. It's enough for me just to get away from everybody."

'Most salmon fishermen are sensible like this. If they'd had no luck I used to tell them to come out of the river and we'd wet the pool – in other words we'd have a wee dram. No Highland gillie would ever refuse a dram.'

William was proud of the fact that his career and that of his predecessor, Hugh White, spanned more than 120 years: 'Yes, that's not a bad record. I took over from old Hugh as head-keeper in 1952 and he'd started the job in the 1880s. That must be something of a record. He was a very old man when I knew him, but he was a very nice man and he really knew the river inside out.'

In winter the gillie's life inevitably slows up unless he has work to do with the stalkers on the hill. But William in latter years had been able to keep busy.

'In winter I toured around towards the end of my time. The fishing ends here on the Beauly on 15 October and for the last week of October I always went to fish the Iythan, a marvellous sea-trout river about 15 miles north of Aberdeen. I got a few days from a Miss Hunter who had the fishing there.

'There's a long wait for the fishing to start again here on the Beauly because although we open on 10 February the river was never worth fishing till July. September and October were the best months in terms of numbers of fish, but July was best for fresh fish. Seven fish in a day was good going at the time of my retirement, but when I was much younger we would expect to get half a dozen out of a single pool in a day.'

William's two daughters – both married to servicemen – come to see him often and he is clearly enjoying his retirement: 'Oh yes I'm enjoying life and I still enjoy going out fishing when I'm booked with particular people, many of whom are really my friends. I only gave it up full time because some of our lochs are 9 miles long and rowing that kind of distance is hard work for a man of my age.'

ANGLING
IN THE ARCHIVES

ooooo

A GIANT LOST

I RECOLLECT ONCE, when spinning under the north shore, not far from the Cut in a deep bay surrounded by walls of bullrushes, suddenly finding that my spinning bait – a whole eel of about ½1b weight – was fast, very fast indeed – in something. From the perfectly passive, yet at the same time utterly unyielding nature of the resistance I concluded I had got hold of a rock or submerged stump, though how such should be found in water which I knew to be 20ft deep at least was somewhat unaccountable.

I had very powerful new gimp tackle, a strong line and a stout rod and I spared neither in my attempts to get clear – still without the slightest signs of the obstacle, whatever it was, giving way.

Suddenly my bait began quietly, perfectly quietly, to move away. 'Hughes,' I shouted to my trusty gillie, 'Hughes, it is a fish. I believe I have hooked Leviathan.' At that moment the line came quietly home without an effort or struggle, and without – the flight. To rig up a fresh flight – this time of double gimp – was the work of a very few minutes and another eel bait, still longer than the first, was soon in the water.

Almost immediately I was fast again in the fish, who pursued precisely the same tactics as before – at first remaining motionless and then after a little while moving off without struggle or emotion. And after a display of about the same amount of vitality as before, once more the line came back to my hand with the double gimp neatly and cleanly severed a few inches above the bait. I fished the water over again, and again the next day, but never saw anything more of my conqueror, unless indeed a vast 'wallow' a few minutes later on the surface of the lough some 80yd away, was an indication he was there and probably trying to rid himself of his recent dinner. What this fish weighed can, of course, only be a matter of conjecture; but I have had some experience of the ways of heavy fish, both pike and salmon, and I have always believed that on that occasion I lost the chance of basketing the biggest pike of my life. These Lough Corrib pike fight like demons. I remember my wife catching one that weighed only 13lb, and in his struggles to make for home – a rush bed about 80yd off – he actually towed the boat a good many yards in that direction before he was basketed. We all thought at first that it must be a salmon from his style of running.

E. Cholmondeley Pennell, Fishing, 1886

PIKE EATS BOY

ONE OF MY SONS, aged fifteen, went with three other boys to bathe in Inglemere Pond, near Ascot racecourse. He walked gently into the water to about the depth of 4ft when he spread out his hands to attempt to swim. Instantly a large fish came up and took his hand into his mouth as far up as the wrist, but, finding he could not swallow it, relinquished his hold, and the boy, turning round, prepared for a hasty retreat out of the pond; his companions, who saw it, also scrambled out of the pond as fast as possible.

My son had scarcely turned himself round when the fish came up behind and immediately seized his other hand crosswise, inflicting some very deep wounds on the back of it. The boy raised his first-bitten and still bleeding arm, and struck the monster a hard blow on the head, then the fish disappeared.

The other boys assisted him to dress, bound up his hand with their handkerchiefs, and brought him home. We took him down to Mr Brown, surgeon, who dressed seven wounds in one hand; and so great was the pain the next day that the lad fainted twice; the little finger was bitten through the nail and it was more than six weeks before it was well. The nail came off and the scar remains to this day.

Reading Mercury, June 1856

AN INFALLIBLE ANOINTMENT FOR FISH BAIT

TAKE OF MAN'S FAT and cat's fat, of each half an ounce; mummy, finely powdered, three drams; cumium seed, finely powdered, one dram; distilled oil of aniseed and spike, of each six drops; civet, two grains; and campline, four grains; make an ointment according to art.

When you angle with this, anoint 8in of line next the hook. Keep it in a pewter box, made something taper; and when you use it never angle with less than two or three hairs next the hook, because if you do and angle with one hair, it will not stick well to the line.

Recommended by M. Charras to Louis XIV, King of France

SEEING EYE TO EYE

A VERY SINGULAR, though I believe not unparalleled instance of the voracity of the perch occurred to me while fishing in Windermere. In removing the hook from the jaws of the fish, one eye was accidentally displaced and remained adhering to it. Knowing the reparative capabilities of piscine organisation, I returned the maimed perch, which was too small for my basket, to the lake, and, being somewhat scant of minnows, threw the line in again with the eye attached as bait – there being no other of any description on the hook.

The float disappeared almost instantly and on landing the newcomer, it turned out to be the fish I had the moment before thrown in, and which had thus been actually caught on his own eye.

H. Cholmondeley Pennell, Perch Fishing, 1886

THE STRANGER ON THE SHORE

WE FISHED FOR YEARS, my Uncle and I, down where the sea met the river and such was the remoteness of the place that never once did we see another man or child crossing the wide flat sands of the estuary. Never, that is, until one year's end long ago.

We had spent the day repairing the house which stood alone, bleached and whitened by centuries of wind and salt. Even the furniture was centuries old by then; it was as old as the house and each piece so heavy and crooked, but each piece a part of our lives.

So we had spent that day repairing the weatherboarding with odd planks that we found washed up on the beach. They made the house look more ramshackle year by year, but since no one else ever saw it what did that matter? When occasionally we stopped to exchange a few words we automatically looked out over the distant waters in case a ship was passing. But it was years since anything had passed this way.

Then, one afternoon, Uncle suggested that we try fishing. It was a bad day for it, too cold and the wind all wrong, but I didn't like to argue with Uncle. We took out the heavy rods and the great brass reels and tramped down to the water's edge. Uncle could cast beautifully and though I watched him for many years I never really learned the art. He threw our lines 80, perhaps 100yd out into the low, angry surf, and then we waited. The thick cane rod tops nodded gently towards the water keeping time with the movement of the waves, but no fish disturbed their rhythm. As usual, we watched out to sea, saying nothing to each other because long silences were our way. If we had spent some time watching back over the flat lands behind us we might have seen the stranger coming. But it would have made no difference. We would have stayed and waited for him because there was nothing else to do.

'Anything doing?'

The voice behind us, not startling, but strong and confident. The owner of the voice wore clothes that appeared to be made from a million layers of rags and scarves and tatters of old coats and jackets. He was almost emaciated, to judge by his face, but he wore so many layers of clothing that he looked like a giant. Uncle and I only stared at him.

'Anything doing?' he said again. 'Perhaps it's not such a good day for fishing. Perhaps you should be home by the fire, with the doors locked against the wind.'

Then, looking at me, he said: 'Try casting that bit closer into the gullies where the poor fish lie to escape the coldest waves.'

'We don't know you,' my uncle almost shouted. He looked at the stranger with undisguised ill-feeling, then he turned and faced back out to sea.

'Your uncle won't take an old man's advice,' said the stranger to me. Not knowing what to say in reply, I said nothing, but I knew something had made Uncle angry. When I reeled in to check my hooks I couldn't resist trying a short cast into the foam – it suited me since I could never hope to compete with a champion caster like my Uncle. Almost as soon as my bait hit the water I caught a fat cod and then another and another.

The stranger watched with a calm face, saying nothing, but all the while watching Uncle's back. Soon I had a basketful of fish, but I couldn't bring myself to thank the stranger in front of my Uncle who, all the while had stayed silent and kept his face to the sea.

Evening was coming in and still we three stood on the edge of the sea as if we were the only people in the world. Then, without a word, Uncle lifted his great rod and reeled in. He had caught nothing. As we packed away our things, the stranger came closer and asked if we would give him a fish. I looked at Uncle, wondering what I should do. He took no notice and packed our fish into his bag.

'Would you give me a fish?' said the stranger once again, but this time directly to my Uncle who, suddenly and without a word, struck the man hard across the face. He fell and as he lay there my Uncle pushed me past him, across the sands and back towards the house.

That night we ate the cod and listened in silence to the wind. In the morning, my Uncle was dead.

Robert Green, Tales of the Sea, 1890

A GILLIE ON THE SEA LOCH

SOME TWENTY YEARS AGO Mr Cholmondeley Pennell and the late Frank Buckland were fishing off Plymouth. Mr Pennell as might be expected, was using a pike rod and a gut paternoster. With this tackle he not only had better sport than Frank Buckland and the boatman, but exceeded the combined takes of his companions and some persons who were in a boat not far distant.

On my first attempt at sea fishing in Scotch waters, a very similar incident occurred. The place was Loch Inchard. A friend and I strolled down from Rhiconich Hotel carrying pike rods. Arriving at the water's edge we met our gillie who looked at us with astonishment and asked what the rods were for.

'To fish with,' I ventured to remark. 'Ye'll no catch fish with rods in the sea loch,' said the gillie most positively. 'No man ever has and no man ever will. It's only the laddies who catch the cuddies from the rocks there with small mussels that use the rods. Ye'll catch all the fish ye need with these hand-lines' pointing to some rough gear lying at the bottom of the boat.

My friend was so impressed that he went to the trouble of taking his rod back to the hotel. I stuck to mine, but I saw that I had fallen in our man's estimation, the worthy fellow eyeing me with a look that plainly said 'A wilful man, maun gae his ain gait.'

A few minutes later we were rowing down the long narrow inlet of the sea, which must have been beautiful indeed before some great glacier swept slowly over it and rounded all the mountaintops.

The anchor was cast a mile or so away from the hotel on the whiting grounds. I used my pike rod and a paternoster made out of a single salmon gut; in fact fished much as I should for perch, but with slightly stronger tackle. There were great quantities of fish in the loch and in a couple of hours a large whiting, grey gurnets, and some remarkably fine plaice had found their way onto the boat. The three hand-lines were worked by my friend and the gillie; each hand-line had two hooks, yet those six hooks in all caught fewer fish than were taken on my two-hook paternoster.

Before we returned to shore the gillie frankly admitted that the rod was 'nae so bad.'

John Bickerdyke, Sea Fishing, 1895

A DIALOGUE BETWEEN A CARP AND A GRAYLING

AT A FISH FESTIVAL, the carp and the grayling quarrelled on a point of precedence. 'I bask in the favour of the great and powerful,' said the carp, 'even man condescends to take care of me and make ponds for my special use and protection.'

'But,' retorted the grayling, 'look at my elegant form and glittering scales. I am much handsomer than you are.' The other fishes commencing to side with the contending parties, a scene of general strife seemed imminent, when the wily old trout restored peace to the company by saying: 'Why should we all be disturbed by this ridiculous quarrel? Let the disputants go to Judge Dolphin, he is a wise and just fish and will soon decide the question.'

So the carp and the grayling went to the dolphin and having laid the case before him he said, 'My children you place me in a very awkward position. I am bound to do you justice, but how can I, never having seen either of you before. While you have been residing in fresh waters, I have been all my life rolling about in the restless waves of the ocean. Consequently I cannot give a conscientious opinion as to which is the best fish, without I first taste you.'

With that, he snapped up the carp and the grayling and, swallowing them down his gullet, he said: No one ought himself to commend above all others, lest he offend.

Dialogus Creaturam Moralizalum, 1480

THE PEARL MAKERS

ITS NAME, BLEAK, which has reference to its shining white scales, is taken from a northern word meaning to bleach or whiten – *blik* (Danish) *blick* (Swedish or German) meaning glance and glimmer.

Its brilliant scales appeared, some years ago, not unlikely to lead to its total extinction. A silvery pigment is found on the undersurface of the scales from which they derive their metallic lustre and this colouring matter was universally used in the bead trade for imparting a pearly tint to their wares.

So great at one time was the demand, when the fashion of wearing imitation pearls was at its height, that the price of a quart measure of scales varied from one or two guineas to five.

At one factory alone, in Paris, 10,000 pearls were issued a week. And when it is considered that each pound of scales cost the lives of four thousand fish and that this pound only produced four ounces of pigment, some estimate of the destruction effected among the bleak may be formed.

The Thames fishermen gave themselves no trouble beyond stripping off these valuable appendages, throwing away the fish when scaled. Roach and dace and some other fish also furnished a colouring substance, though of an inferior quality.

The method of obtaining and using the pigment was first, by washing and then scraping the scales until the colouring matter descended to the bottom of the vessel in the form of a pearly precipitate, whence it was removed by small tubes and injected into thin hollow glass beads of various sizes.

It occasionally happens to the angler to catch pearls ready made. These are found in the large river-mussel which, as is well known, will not infrequently swallow a worm or other ground bait, taking so fast a hold with its shell lips as to be fairly hoisted out of the river's bed and basketed.

An instance recently occurred near Tweed Mill, Coldstream, where a boy, who was worm fishing for trout in the Chapel Brook, caught a mussel 4in long and 2in broad, containing no less than forty fine pearls of different sizes, some of which were thought to be worth 1 shilling each.

H. Cholmondeley Pennell, Fishing, 1886

CASTING AT THE SAVOY

Two Americans staying in London in the early fifties had an argument over whether or not it would be possible to cast a fly from the roof of their hotel – the Savoy – over the gardens and the busy Embankment and into the Thames.

They were so determined to settle the dispute that they went along to Hardy Brothers, the tackle-makers, and asked them to decide if such a thing was possible. Hardy Brothers approached Esmond Drury who agreed to attempt the feat on condition that he was tied securely to a chimney on the hotel roof.

Early one Sunday morning and with the help of a policeman who stopped all the traffic on the Embankment, he proved that it was indeed possible to cast a fly into the Thames from the roof of the Savoy.

THE GILLIE'S WIFE

I walked out one morning to see the spot where I had hooked a fine sea trout and the tale is worth recording, showing how I gained by having a waterkeeper's wife on my side.

I had got up early as there had been a nice spate and everything was perfection. About the second cast I was in him, the trout making several desperate leaps and runs, getting over a ridge of gravel into another pool and from which I felt I could never get him back and knew that he had me beat.

The road and the river abutted and just at this moment a country woman came along and bid me the time of day, and after looking at me playing the trout saw the predicament I was in. She said it was a bad business and asked if the fish was any size. I told her, as far as I could tell from 3 to 4lb.

Then she made this proposal: that she would take the rod and play the fish and when he was beat I might get a chance at him with the landing net. That was agreed at once; it was the only chance and not much of a one at that.

The woman took the rod out of my hands and I saw at once it was not the first time that she had played a trout. I proceeded to drop down from the wall into about 3ft of water running pretty swiftly, wading across to the far side of the stream. The fish could see me quite plainly and every time I approached it fled from one end of the pool to the other.

The trout was now showing signs of being tired and his big, golden-looking body shining through the brown peaty water made me think that he might be a bigger one than I thought at first.

Here the good lady gave him the butt and led him beautifully up to and into the net. Such a beauty! I had to wade back to the river wall; everything my lady friend did was with precision; the

ANGLING APPARATUS—No. 1.

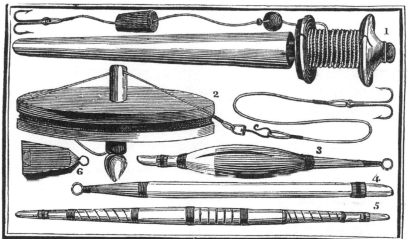

1. Bank runner.
2. Cork or man-of-war trimmer.
3. Cork float.
4. Plug float.
5. Tip-capped float.
6. Plummet to take the depth.

way she wound up the line and laid the rod on the top of the wall reel up, then reached down for the handle of the landing-net, pulling it up safely to the road, while I got out of the river bed. I had not scales with me, but on my return to my room was able to record that this sporting fish pulled the scales at 5lb good.

I thanked the good woman for having helped me and made her come in and have some breakfast and congratulated her on the masterful manner in which she played the fish. In reply she said, 'Your honour, what about it? I have played scores and scores of them in my time. Isn't my husband head waterkeeper up by?' meaning of the district.

If all the waterkeepers and their wives were such good sportsmen and women, there would be better fishing and I would never begrudge them a fish.

S. B. Wilkinson, *Reminiscences of Sport in Ireland*, 1931

LITERATURE OF THE SEA

NEVER ON SALMON RIVER or trout stream have I enjoyed more splendid fly fishing than has fallen to my lot from Filey Brigg. Sometimes so eager were the fish that if one missed the fly another was hooked immediately afterwards. It was simply a fight against time and a rising tide.

The enthusiastic sea-fisher may claim for the sea the first place in the variety of sport afforded, but he must admit that, on its literary side it is a very bad second in its rivalry with river and lake.

From the time of Izaak Walton, freshwater fishing has been the subject of a series of most charming works, some of them, in parts, almost prose poems. And a fascination, I may say glamour, has been cast over trout, salmon and other fish which will remain until English angling literature is forgotten.

Sea fish and sea fishing, notwithstanding their national importance, have a very small niche indeed in our literature, probably because until the middle of this century the coarseness of the tackle commonly used deterred most anglers, so many of whom are men of refined literary tastes.

John Bickerdyke, Sea Fishing, 1895

NEVER ON A SUNDAY

TWO ANGLERS – BOTH SASSENACHS – had waited at Loch Awe for a breeze for a whole week and waited in vain. On the sabbath morn there was a glorious ripple; the kind of ripple in which a trout rushes madly at the angler's fly. Fish these anglers must. But the gillie was an elder of the kirk and he turned up the whites of his eyes when they suggested he should just let them have the boat for an hour or two.

'I could nae do it, such a thing has no been done on the loch within the memory o' man.'

They offered untold bribes of silver and gold, but the gillie was obdurate, until his eyes rested on the gold sovereign held out to him.

'Nae, nae,' he said. 'I'll nae let the boat. I'm an elder of the kirk ye ken, and a God-fearing man and it's no reasonable to expect me to consent to such a wicked proceeding, but the boat lies there in the rushes and the oars are in her. Just ye gang away doon and get in her and row awa oot the lake and I'll come doon and swear at ye, but ye must take no notice of what I say. Just row away and I'll call for the money the morn.'

The Angler, 1899

A PEA-SHOOTER AND A BLUEBOTTLE

HE WAS AN OLD and wise fish, and had his headquarters opposite a clubhouse on a certain famous stream. Many a fly had passed over his venerable head. Once long ago it is said that he was hooked on a piece of bread, but quickly wound the line round a stump, extracted the hook and was rising to some natural flies half an hour later. New members used to bet that they would catch him. The old members took their bets and their money and obtained satisfaction out of the fish that way. It was an aggravating feature in that trout's behaviour that nothing would put him down short of a cart rope thrown over his head. He was as tame as a pug dog, but had the cunning, without the wildness, of a hawk.

One day there joined the club a man who was not an expert with the fly rod. He, like the rest, said he thought he could catch the trout. The old members laughed and took his bets, as was their custom with newcomers. A mean thing this, but very much the way of the world.

It was August. One sultry evening the new member came to the club armed with a pea shooter and many bluebottles. Was he going to catch the trout with a pea-shooter? No, he was only going to begin to catch him – the operation might take some time.

Deftly a half-dead bluebottle was puffed out of the tube in front of the fish. It was taken, of course, as everything eatable from a trout's point of view was taken. The fish had a rare supper that evening.

The following day the new member repeated the operation. He fed the fish in this manner for more than a week; the others smiled and looked on.

'I will catch him soon,' said the new member. 'I am only waiting for wind.'

At the end of three weeks there came a day when a stiff breeze was blowing upstream. It was the day on which the catastrophe was fated to happen. The new member appeared at the clubhouse with a long slender rod, on which was arranged running tackle and a length of fine, but strong gut, terminating with a single hook.

He took his stand some distance below the fish, and began feeding him as usual. On the hook was a bluebottle. Good luck helped our friend who, however, exhibited considerable skill. The upstream breeze took the hooked fly just over the trout, and the new member let it fall and at the same time puffed out a fly from the tube.

Which would the trout take? It was an anxious moment. Had the rod been in front instead of behind him, he would have taken neither. But he did not see the rod, having no eyes in his tail (this has been questioned) and the fly containing the hook was sucked in. How he fought.

Was the wisdom of twenty years to culminate in destruction by means of a pea shooter and a bluebottle? Where was that invaluable stump? The new member had removed it. The weeds? They had been recently cut. A leap for liberty then? That made matters worse for the gut got wound round his body and hampered him sadly. But let fall the curtain. He died – as wise and grand and noble a specimen as has ever been seen in a trout stream.

John Bickerdyke, Days of My Life, 1895

ILL MET BY MOONLIGHT

ONE MORNING OLD DAWKINS came to me and asked me to watch with him next night for an otter that haunted the mere, and I promised to do so, as the old fellow made rather a point of it.

I had been a good deal disturbed in my mind, for Lucy had missed that very morning a handsome snake bracelet, which went twice round the arm and clasped at the head and tail, the head glittering with diamonds, rubies and emeralds. It was a very handsome bracelet, which she had worn the night before and now, though they searched high and low, it could not be found. It was most extraordinary; we could not account for it. Night came, however, and we sought a little bothy which Dawkins had made near the edge of the mere.

'Master Fred,' said he as we sat watching in the moonlight, 'Mr Fred,' he said in solemn tones, 'I fear's I be'nt long for this world.'

'Why, what on earth do you mean, Dawkins?' I asked. 'I seed the white lady last night sir, as ever wor; and they as does that don't never live very long after, they says.' 'White lady be blowed! What nonsense. You saw a shadow, or a wreath of mist, or something of that sort.' 'That I didn't sir, I see her as plain as I see you now. She came along the shore there over the far side, and went on to the jetty to the end and stood on the very brink and waved her hand over the water as if trying to cast something from her. Then she wrung her hands and gradually disappeared in the trees. But hist. What's that?' There was a splash some 60yd away and evidence of a severe struggle as we saw the otter come up to the surface, fighting fiercely with a big pike. Now the pike pulled the otter under; now the otter got him to the surface. It was a desperate encounter, but the fish seemed to get weaker and weaker as they drew nearer and nearer to the bank and finally the otter scrambled ashore with his prey about 30yd off us. When we got to them both otter and pike were dead. We took them and carried them to Dawkins' cottage, and I returned to mine. The next morning, before I was down, old Dawkins came to me in a great hurry.

'What do you think Mr Fred? As I was a-cleaning out that there big pike I found this here in his innards.' And he produced a beautiful snake bracelet, set with rubies, diamonds and emeralds which I recognised at once as Lucy's. While turning it over a sudden thought struck me and bidding him be silent and say nothing of the discovery, I determined to watch for myself for a night or two. Then stationing myself in a low boathouse close to the jetty, I did so.

The first night I had my watch for nothing. The second night I was sitting in the boat and had almost fallen asleep when a light footstep on the gravel path which leads to the jetty, struck on my ear and I became all attention instantly as a female figure in a white robe-de-chambre walked on to the jetty and going to the end, stretched out her arms over the water. Something glistened in her hand under the moonbeams, and in a low tone she murmured, 'Fairy, fairy tell me true, Does my sweetheart dwell with you?' As she spoke these words she dropped the glittering object into the water and it disappeared with a slight splash; then she turned round and I saw the face of Lucy in a state of somnambulism. She came slowly down the jetty and disappeared into the trees. The next day I apprised her father of the circumstance; he had the spit well dredged and they recovered a great deal of missing jewellery. Master pikey must have seen the bracelet as it fell through the water in the moonlight and grabbed it as a delicacy.

Francis Francis, Angling Reminiscences, 1887

AN EXHIBITION OF MONSTERS

I QUIETLY CHUCKLED TO myself when I heard our hostess whisper to her husband something to the effect that there was no fish in the house, and indeed very little for dinner, so he must take the boat and go out with his man, Malone, and get a trout or two. He said that could 'easily' be done – a fatal remark so far as he was concerned. Being usually glad of an excuse to go fishing, I begged to join in the search after trout and Mr– lent me one of his boats.

Leaving my friend to fish round a little bay, I voyaged off with my man to the opposite point, where I had often seen large trout rising. I was most careful to expect nothing, in fact, I assured Andy who was rowing me, that it was a practical impossibility that we should catch anything, but we would just try.

It took us some twenty minutes to make the point, and by that time a slight favouring ripple, which might have helped us to a fish, had died away. Dark clouds were gathering and just as we reached our fishing ground I heard distant thunder rumbling along the mountains. Then happened one of the strangest things I have ever seen in my life as a fisherman. A few fine spots of rain began to fall and with them came down swarms of small black flies. Hardly had these touched the water before, all around us, enormous trout began to show themselves and

ANGLING APPARATUS—No. 2.

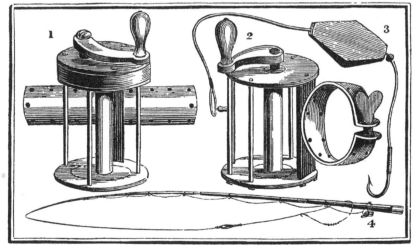

1. Multiplying Winch.
2. Common Winch.
3. Leger Line and Hook.

4. Rod, Winch, Running Line, Float and Hook, for Barbel, Perch, Carp, &c.

swim about with their back fins out of the water, which were powdering it.

When I first saw this remarkable exhibition of monsters, I certainly thought I should quickly catch a big trout. So long as that was my state of mind not a fish would look at my flies which, it must be admitted, were a trifle large for use in calm water. But as hope departed, and I began to realise that I was doomed to failure that evening, so apparently did my chances increase.

When I had absolutely given up all hope, a fish, doubtless feeling that my despondency merited some reward, rose to one of my flies and gave me as fine a piece of sport as any I had experienced in that lake. Before he was in the landing-net the extraordinary rise of large trout was over.

John Bickerdyke, Wild Sport in Ireland, 1897

SEA-FISHING SUPERSTITIONS

CERTAIN BUCKIE FISHERMEN DRESSED up an unfortunate barrel-maker in a flannel shirt with bars all about it and wheeled him through the town in a barrel. The herring fisheries have been very bad and it was supposed that this proceeding would improve them. There are even dark stories of men and women being burnt for having cast their evil eye on the fishery and driven away the herrings.

In Norfolk there was a curious theory that herrings and fleas made their appearance about the same time. A fisherman of Cromer was credited with the following remark: 'Lawks Sir, times is as you might look in my flannel shirt and scarce see a flea and then there ain't but a few herring; but times that'll be right alive with them and there's certain to be a sight of fish.'

And then the Manx fishermen who are particularly superstitious think there is a great virtue in taking out a dead wren to sea. The idea appears to be based on an old tradition of some sea spirit which haunted the herring fisheries and brought storms. Assuming the form of a wren it would fly away, carrying with it bad weather and misfortune.

John Bickerdyke, Sea Fishing, 1895

BRANDY AS A FISH REVIVER

I HAVE CONTINUED MY experiments in relation to brandy as a means of restoring life to a dying fish, the results being, in the main, highly satisfactory.

It was highly interesting to see the plucky manner a trout battled with his fainting condition, after a dose of brandy, and came out the conqueror.

Strange to say, the salmon did not once attempt to rouse himself after being dosed, the consequence being fatal to him. This was the only fish that succumbed under the treatment.

As regards the dace, I had him out of the water three times of five minutes each. He was exceedingly faint and almost dead, but immediately the brandy was given he pulled himself together and in the course of a few minutes not only recovered, but darted around with a rapidity positively amazing.

The Fishing Gazette, 1884

HOOK IN THE HAND

I HAD A GOLDEN OLIVe fly on the tail and a Lough Gill on the drop and up he came directly we reached the lodge, making a tremendous ring where his tail hit the water going down. In him right enough and the Golden Olive had done the trick. He was a sporting fish and fought hard, but gradually his runs were getting shorter and his jumps fewer.

Gradually he came nearer, the net was in Pat's right hand with

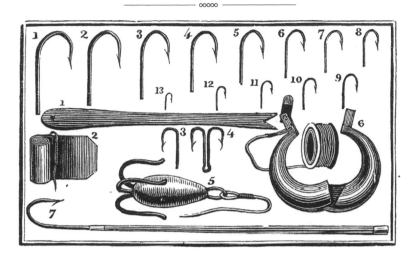

his left hand resting on the stern of the boat. Suddenly the fish made a terrific plunge right under the boat and dragged the dropper onto poor Pat's hand – the hook entered the fleshy part between thumb and finger. It all happened like a flash. Pat never flinched.

He seized the hook and literally tore it away from the flesh, and there seemed to be at least 6in of stretched skin before the hook gave away. It was a horrible sight and must have caused Pat great pain, but he did not seem to feel any. It was soon all over and a beautiful fresh twelve-pounder lay on the boards at the bottom of the boat. The evening was closing in rapidly, but there was still enough light to show to all the anglers collected on the bridge that we had a clean bright fish.

Next morning when Pat arrived he asked me to examine the Lough Gill fly as his hand had given him much pain during the night and he thought that there must be a piece of the hook left there. Sure enough the greater part of the hook was broken off and no doubt in his hand. I sent Pat off home at once with

instructions to his wife to put on a big poultice, and after a couple of days the wound joined to heal, broke and the piece of
hook was removed. The wound was kept clean and, aided by
some healing ointment, he was fit for work in a few days.

S. B. Wilkinson, Reminiscences of Sport in Ireland, 1931

PIKE MADNESS

Now there is nothing remarkable about seeing a rod and reel
in Ireland, but these particular weapons made me open my
eyes and mouth in amazement. The rod at its point was thick as
my little finger, the reel not less than 8in in diameter, and the
line – shades of Izaak Walton! What a line was there. I have
towed a canoe up the Thames with cord less thick.

I was on the point of enquiring into the particular uses of this
remarkable tackle, when the door of the cabin opened and a short,
wiry old man with deep set, piercing eyes, iron-grey hair and clad
in a shabby suit of tweeds, came in wearily, bearing just another
rod and reel, and a huge basket which I instinctively felt contained
fish. He took no notice of me, but gasped out, in a voice which told
of his exhausted condition: 'The steelyard, the steelyard.'

With trembling hands he opened the rush basket and turned out
of it one of the largest pike I had ever seen. Mrs O'Day who
seemed in no way surprised, produced an ancient rusty instrument
and proceeded in a businesslike manner to weigh the fish. The old
man's excitement while she did this was painful to witness.

'Is it? Is it?' he commenced. 'No, it isn't,' said Mrs O'Day
calmly. 'He's 5lb short.'

I was looking at the fish, but, hearing a groan, turned my eyes
to the old fisherman and saw him lying on the floor of the shebeen. He had fainted.

'Poor ould man,' said Mrs O'Day. 'It's disappointed he is and weak too for devil a bit of food has he touched this day since yesterday. Undo his collar sir, and I'll mix him a timperance drink.'

And so her tongue ran on. Meanwhile the old fellow came to himself and sat up, but his eyes went at once to the pike, which still lay on the floor.

'Only 35lb,' I heard him mutter to himself. 'But I will have him soon. I will have him soon now.'

Mrs O'Day's 'timperance' drink was in the nature of an egg flip. It acted like a charm on the old man, who five minutes after drinking it rose, kicked the fish to the side of the cabin and for the first time appeared to be aware that a stranger was in the shebeen. Mrs O'Day noticed the questioning look he cast at me.

'It's a gentleman who lost his way in the bog,' she said. 'Not fishing?' he asked rather anxiously.

'No, snipe shooting,' said I, and he seemed to me greatly relieved at the intelligence.

Mrs O'Day now turned out the stew on to a large dish and apologised for having no plates, remarking that she was 'not used to the gentry'. We were both of us more or less famished and talked but little during the meal, after which Mrs O'Day having provided us with a second edition of the 'timperance' drink, we drew the settle close to the peat fire, and commenced to chat over our pipes.

My new acquaintance, from what I could gather, was an Englishman who had lived for many years in Ireland and apparently passed his whole time in fishing. But I was able to tell him of certain modern methods of pike fishing of which he had heard nothing. By and by he began to get communicative and finally I ventured to ask him why the weighing of the pike had so disturbed him. Without hesitation he told me the following story.

'From a boy I was an enthusiastic fisherman. I need not trouble to tell you how I caught salmon in Norway, trout in the Test, and enormous grayling in the Hampshire Avon. I fished whenever and wherever I could and nothing, however large or however small, came amiss to me. But one thing I had never caught – a really large pike. Even in Sweden I never took one over 30lb. This nettled me, for many were the tales I read of monsters, particularly in the Irish lakes.

'One morning I read in a sporting paper a letter from an Irishman - a tackle dealer so I afterwards ascertained - asking why English anglers did not come more over there. In the lakes in his neighbourhood there was fine pike fishing. Thirty-pounders were common, and they got a forty-pounder or two every season. Here was exactly the information I wanted. I told some friends about it, but they only smiled. I said I would catch a forty-pounder before long. They replied that there was no such thing as a forty-pounder, alive or stuffed. Well, the end of it was I made a bet that I would go to Ireland and before I returned I would catch a fish of that weight.'

I here interrupted his story to tell him of a strange coincidence. It was that very tacklemaker's letter which had first brought me to Ireland. 'But go on,' I said, 'finish your story and then you shall have mine.'

'I began badly,' he continued, 'I wrote to the man for details of these loughs he mentioned and received a reply from his widow, he having died soon after writing the paragraph. From the poor woman I could get no information. She said she had no idea to which waters her husband referred; in fact, she knew of none. Then I put a letter of enquiry in the sporting papers and received many replies from persons, some of whom were possibly not altogether disinterested in the matter.'

'I have suffered in the same way myself,' I interjected. 'I

came to Ireland armed with tackle such as would hold the largest pike that ever lived.' He continued, not noticing my interruption. 'At first I was hopeful. What tales they told me to be sure. There was one of the big pike caught in Lough Derg or, I should say, was killed by some workmen who were digging drains near the lake. The bishop of Killaloe was reputed to be fond of the pike, and to him the fish was taken. It was so large that half its body dragged on the ground as two men carried it, slung on a pole, to the bishop's palace. When the bishop saw it, he told them to give it to the pigs. "I am fond of pike," said he, "but distinctly decline to have anything to do with sharks." Ah! What would I not have given to have caught that fish.'

'Well, I fished here and I fished there, first trying all the large Shannon Lakes, and then visiting Corrib and Cullen. Thence I went to the north of Ireland, catching now and then some fine fish, but never even a thirty-pounder. The more difficult I found it to attain my object, the more determined I became to succeed. And I shall succeed yet. Let me see. It is now twenty-five years since I came to Ireland. I must have caught thousands of pike in that time – that one there on the floor is the largest of the lot; in fact, the largest I have seen caught by myself or anybody else. This is my second great disappointment. At Athlone I thought I had succeeded. That was a big fish. I took him to the station and weighed him there. "Forty-three pounds," said the station master.

'A Major Brown who was looking on began to prod the fish with his stick. "Something hard there," he said. "Let's cut him open and see what he had for dinner."

'I would not agree to this as I wanted the skin entire, but the major squeezed him a bit and up came a lot of swan shot which my scoundrel of a boatman had evidently poured down his throat so that he might earn the reward I had promised him if I caught a heavy fish.

'But at last I really have found a monster pike - the catching of him is only a question of time. Not a quarter of a mile from this cabin (here he lowered his voice to a whisper) is a deep reedy lake. The priest has a boat on it, which he lends me. I was rowing along the other evening when something struck the boat with such force that I was thrown from the seat and nearly capsized. It was in deep water and there are no rocks in the lake. I had rowed right on to a pike as large as a calf.'

He said the last sentence slowly and earnestly. I expect I showed great interest in the statement for, like the old man, it had long been my ambition to catch a really immense pike.

'Well,' said I, 'let us go and try the lake together. I should like to help you land such a monster.'

'Ah, but you might catch him and not I. How then?' And he gave me a very unpleasant look out of his deep-set eyes.

We said nothing for a while, when my companion suddenly startled me by asking if I was aware that he was the Emperor of Germany. I said I was not, and another unpleasant silence ensued.

Mrs O'Day had made up two heather beds for us on the mud floor and without undressing we each stretched ourselves on our moorland couches.

Just as I was dropping off to sleep, my companion got up on his elbow and said gravely: 'Hang me if I don't believe you are a pike. I'll have a triangle into you tomorrow morning. Good night.'

There was no doubt about it. He was mad. I dared not go to sleep. I made a pretence of it until the old man began to snore and then sat by the fire until daybreak when, leaving some money on the table for Mrs O'Day, I sped away over the moor.

Years afterwards I was telling the tale of the demented angler who, I felt certain, had lost his wits in his unavailing search after a big Irish pike when I was interrupted by Rooney, of the Irish Bar, who burst into a peal of laughter, swearing that he knew my pike-fishing acquaintance well and that there was no saner man in Ireland.

'Fact is Johnny,' said he, ' the old boy was fearful you would get that big fish before him and so he thought he would frighten you home.'

Rooney may say what he likes, but I decline to believe in the sanity of any man who expatriates himself during a quarter of a century in the endeavour to catch a 40lb pike.

John Bickerdyke, Wild Sports in Ireland, 1895

THE OBSTINATE GILLIE

A S A GENERAL RULE, however, a stranger to the river, when first fishing it, must follow implicitly the advice of the gillie, if he wishes for sport, as these men know of every hole and corner where fish are wont to lie, though they are often much astonished when a fish is taken in any other part of the river.

I was fishing in the Lochy in the autumn, and I hooked a fish in a part of the river usually only frequented by sea trout. As my line tightened and I felt the fish, I said 'Duncan, he's a fish.' 'No sir,' said Duncan, 'I don't think it, only a trout. I never saw a fish rise there.'

Well, his manner of running and tugging made me doubt, but Duncan was obstinate and persisted that 'only trout rose there', but gradually he wakened up. 'I think it is a fish whatever, and he's bigger than I thought. Perhaps you had better get out of the boat.' As I wound up he again sung out 'only a big trout'. 'No, Duncan, a fish I'll bet' and sure enough as we got him into shallow water, Duncan had to give up and gaff a beautiful fresh-run fish of 7lb. 'Well,' he said, 'I never saw a fish take there before.'

Two curious instances of what may be called singular vagaries of salmon were related to me by a friend, a first-rate salmon-fisher. He was fishing in the Ribble in what is called the Froth Pot, close to Mytton Hall and the Mytton riverkeeper was netting Clay Hole, a pool about ⅓ mile above, and as is usual in that country, beating the water with poles to drive the fish. All at once having made a cast toward the opposite and deep side of the pool, he heard a violent splashing and hubbub on the shingle behind him and turning round found that a fine 15lb fresh-run salmon driven, as he supposed, and still supposes, by the netters above, had, in his rush downstream run himself high and dry.

The same friend on another occasion was fishing the Laxford; he had fished the pool above and while casting into what is called the Duchess Pool, became aware of the presence above him on the river of a large bird, which he believed to be a great northern diver, and which appeared to be doing something on the river, which, at the distance he was, could not make out.

Presently the bird, which had then apparently caught sight of him, flew off, and my friend continuing his fishing downstream was absent from the spot for some hours. In the evening, returning with his rod on his shoulder, he was surprised to see in midstream, about the spot where he had noticed the bird, the tail of a large salmon well out of the water, and moving slowly to and fro.

Watching this for some time and seeing nothing of the body of the fish, he determined to wade into the stream, about 3ft deep and get close to him if possible. This he succeeded in doing. Still the undulatory motion went on, and he could then plainly make out that the head of the fish was close against the bottom, and that it neither moved nor appeared conscious of his presence.

After looking at it for some moments he gaffed it and carried it out struggling, but faintly and quite unlike a fish suddenly gaffed. On the other hand the fish seemed to have nothing else the matter with him; he was as bright as silver, in perfect condition and had no marks upon him as if he had been injured or struck.

To this day he is quite at a loss to account for the incident, but the impression made upon him was, that the state of the fish was in some way or another connected with the bird.

Edward Hamilton, Recollections of Fly Fishing, 1884

THE POACHER'S BOAST

THIS CASE AGAINST Samuel Beesley, Sampson Beesley, Adam Beesley, Abel Beesley, William Beesley and Richard Allen for poaching with nets upon the Thames at Port Meadow, Oxford, was heard on Tuesday last the 8th inst at the Oxford Petty Sessions, before James Hughes Esq, mayor, in the chair and a very full bench of ten magistrates.

The magistrates adjourned for half an hour, and returned into court, when the mayor said: 'We have earnestly considered the merits of this case throughout and have unanimously determined to convict each one of the defendants. We are much obliged to you for your intimation that the conservators did not wish to press for a heavy penalty. We therefore fine each of the defendants 1s; the defendant Samuel Beesley 15s 6d, costs, in addition, and each of the other defendants the sum of 8s 6d costs. But ... if you have occasion to bring any of them again before us, we can assure you that they will be severely punished.'

Extra watchers are to be placed upon the water at night, the nets being still in possession of the poachers, and old Jem Beesley, the leader of the gang, but who was not of the party on the occasion in question, shouting out at the entrance to the court, in the hearing of Venables, myself and others, that they would go to work at once and d—— all the magistrates, the conservators and the fines; he had got enough to buy up half the lot.

The Field, 1870

PROFESSOR TURNED POACHER

THERE WAS NO CHANCE of recovering the soft, black flappy thing – his hat – which had been whirled into the centre of the stream, and was hurrying seaward.

As a more or less efficient substitute, he took out his red pocket handkerchief, knotted up the four corners and placed it on his head. There was a slight mist falling, which caused him to turn up the collar of his coat, quite hiding the professorial white shirt-front and black tie. The yellow mud, from his feet up to above the knees, the shell jacket – for so the garment appeared with the tails in hiding – these, combined with his curious head-gear, gave him a most extraordinary not to say villainous appearance. But he did not expect to meet anybody and, having come to see the salmon spawn, would not turn back yet a while.

Skirting the foot of a little cliff, which rose abruptly at a bend of the river, he came suddenly on a rough-looking man standing on the rocks well out in the stream, and apparently attempting to hit something with a long stick which he had in his hand.

'Ah,' thought the professor, 'this must be one of my cousin's men salmon fishing.'

The man in the river was awkwardly placed. He would have given a great deal to have been able to run away. But between him and liberty – represented in this case by the opposite bank – was some deep swift water, and he had the choice of return-ing to dry land at the spot where stood the professor, or run the risk of being drowned. The former was the lesser evil of the two and after a while he suddenly jumped from rock to rock and landed on the bank by the side of the learned man.

'Well, have you caught any salmon?'

The man, prepared to run for it, was somewhat reassured by the friendly tones of the professor's voice, and judging from his appearance that he was perhaps of that class which does not bear the poacher any ill-will, replied that he had so far been unsuccessful, but thought that higher up the river there was a chance of getting a big fish. The professor pricked up his ears. Here was an opportunity not to be missed.

'I will give you,' he said, 'I will give you 5, 7, no 10 shillings if you will enable me to hook a salmon. I very much want to catch one.'

The man gazed at him in amazement. Who could this be who

SPORTING INTELLIGENCE.

Native (to Sportsman, at close of a blank afternoon).

"I SEE A TIDY GUDGEON, ABOUT TWO MOILE FURDER DOWN, NOT MORE'N A WEEK AGO!"

offered gold to be shown how to break the law? However, the half sovereign was worth having.

He led his companion to a broad shallow where a pair of large fish were spawning, lent him his cleek and, after giving very careful instructions how it should be used, helped the Professor of Comparative Anatomy to gaff and haul on to the bank a twenty-pounder. The good man, absolutely ignorant of his wrongdoing and the canons of sport, was delighted. Eggs were dropping from the fish, and these he commenced examining carefully through a pocket microscope. He forgot the mud bath, the loss of his hat and his wet feet.

Suddenly his companion caught hold of his arm and pulled him behind a rock.

'They're after us,' he exclaimed.

'Who?' asked the professor, opening his eyes very wide.

'The police.'

'Why?' asked the professor, and during the succeeding fifteen seconds he learned to his horror that he had committed a serious offence against the fishery laws of Scotland. The man suggested that the two should steal across the moor by different ways, as they were almost certain to be discovered if they remained behind the rock.

The professor, less fearful of the law than that his innocent poaching practices should ever become known to the Fishery Board, or in his university, took to his heels and ran. The police soon viewed him and gave hot chase. If he had been a better runner he would probably have been caught, but being quite unused to the rough country over which he was passing, he very soon tripped up, fell and to his surprise found himself sinking through the heather into a very convenient hiding place between two big rocks. His first impulse was to arise and continue his flight, his second to stop where he was. In this he was wise.

The police, like greyhounds, running by sight rather than by scent passed within a couple of yards of him and were soon a mile distant. He lay there for an hour and then, in the darkness, he somehow groped his way back to the lodge. On the way he had to endure many a fall and not a few immersions into icy pools of water. His garments were rent with thorns, his spectacles were broken, his hair was dishevelled and his face was scratched. On the whole he was a very poor specimen of a professor by the time he reached Glenfynandhuloch.

Afraid that the police had preceded him, he hid himself in the byre where Sandy Macdonald found him. He confessed his sins, was put to bed and lay ill at the lodge for a week. Then he went back to his university. He declined the post of scientific advisor to the Fishery Board, and now never passes a fishmonger's shop without a shudder.

John Bickerdyke, Days of My Life, 1895

MACKEREL DECOYS

ACCORDING TO AELIAN, the fishermen of his time trained mackerel to decoy their fellows into a net, just as a little dog is used to lead wild ducks into the hoop-net of the wildfowler.

These remarkable fish would head a shoal and lead it into the nets, which were already spread. More than this, the progeny of these decoys would inherit the same remarkable powers.

Then there is another story of a Norwegian sailor who went bathing, when a shoal of hungry mackerel surrounded and nibbled and worried him until by gentle persistence they worked him some distance out to sea. Assistance came in the shape of men in a boat, but it was with some difficulty that the poor fellow was lifted on board and he was in such a state of exhaustion from loss of blood that he soon died.

Another charming story was once told by Lacepede. On the coast of Greenland are certain shallow bays which are almost landlocked. The water is clear and the bottom of mud. There, throughout the winter, thousands of mackerel might be seen with their heads stuck in the mud and their tails pointing skywards. When they resumed the normal position, their eyesight was affected and they were netted without difficulty.

John Bickerdyke, Sea Fishing, 1895

RUNNING IN THEIR HUNDREDS

A T TIMES WHEN FISH are running up fresh from the sea it is wonderful what freaks they are up to; throwing themselves upwards or sideways, turning somersaults, making tremendous rushes and yet not sporting a bit.

One evening on the Lochy I was returning from the upper part of No 6 beat to have one more cast over the Sloggan when just above the Fox Hunter's cottage the river became suddenly about in all directions. I waded in and cast over hundreds; not a fish would come at the fly, but they would, in their jumps, hit the line often enough.

After a change or two of flies I gave it up and went on my way to the Sloggan. The first cast there with the same fly I had endeavoured to entice the running fish with, I hooked and landed a bright, fresh-run salmon of 10lb.

Edward Hamilton, Recollections of Fly Fishing, 1884

THE DEAD DONKEY

T HE LATE RAINS HAD no effect whatever on the water at Hampton on the 11th. The groundbait could easily be seen in 7ft of water. On this day a good many punts were out, but with the exception of two gentlemen who were fishing with Moses Fulker in the Bough Stream facing the lock at Sunbury, I did not hear of any take worth relating between Molesey Lock and Sunbury Weir.

Myself and friend tried Hampton Deep, the Lower Pile, the Cherry Orchard Swim and back to the Deep a second time. But all was blank, neither roach, dace or barbel would bite and the day's sport saw us with only two perch and some dozen roach and dace.

Mr E, one of the gentlemen with Moses Fulker, lost a good barbel after playing him an hour and a quarter. This party, who took some 30lb of fish, were the only fishermen on this part of the river who had any sport.

During the week but few punts have been out in the Hampton and Sunbury district and I have heard of but one haul worth recording.

It appears that the water bailiffs and riverkeepers are under orders to collect any dead cats, dogs or other offensive animals they may see floating down the river, bring them ashore, and bury them.

A week ago a strange object was seen going downstream. It lodged opposite the water works at Hampton. The riverkeepers were fetched and the stranger was discovered to be that rare animal – a dead donkey. After some trouble it was got on shore and buried with funeral honours.

While speaking of the dead ass and its propinquity to the water works, I might suggest that the sewage from the houses at Sunbury is even more deleterious to health than the dead cats and donkeys. And it is certainly desirable that something should be done to stop such an outflow of filth as I saw there a few days since.

The Field, 1870

HOW CAN ANY WATER BE PRESERVED?

THE KEEPER ON A portion of the River Arrow, a tributary of the Lugg which runs near Leominster and which is preserved by a club, caught four men netting early on a Sunday morning.

Three of the men escaped, but not before he recognised them; the other (a notorious poacher) remained and resisted the keeper who, however, succeeded in taking from him the nets they had been using.

The men were summoned and brought up before the magistrates for poaching, when they received the penalty of a fine of a few shillings and the keeper was told that he had taken the law too much into his own hands by depriving the man of his nets. Is not this an extraordinary decision and how can any water be preserved under these circumstances?

The Field, 1870

SALMON DUET

MR G. ROBINSON OF Seal House, Hexham, when fishing in Alnwick Grange Water on Saturday last, almost simultaneously hooked two salmon. The dropper fly was first taken by a fish apparently of 14 or 15lb which took the fly near the surface of the water and on going down with it brought the stretcher fly to the surface when a larger fish sprang out of the water and seized it.

Both fish ran a considerable distance up the stream when the one at the stretcher repeatedly leapt out of the water, making each time a complete somersault, being pulled back, head first, by the other fish. When they turned back, running down the water, the one on the dropper got free and Mr Robinson joyfully exclaimed: 'I will get the larger one.' The larger fish, after a struggle of twenty-minutes duration was brought to the side and was successfully netted by a gentleman who was fortunately present at the time. It was subsequently measured by a member of the Hexham Angling Club and found to be 39in long, 18½in round and weighed 19lb.

The Field, 1870

HERRING ON THE FLY

O N THE UNIMPEACHABLE AUTHORITY of a Dublin magistrate – Mr Porter – a fly fisher once took a large number of herrings in Dublin Bay.

There was a fish hooked at almost every cast and the fly was a black hackle or black palmer. A gentleman who writes under the name 'Storm Petrel', on the other hand, caught a very large number of herrings with a fly dressed to represent a red caterpillar, and on another with a green body, these hooking fish better than the ordinary Irish herring fly, which has white wings and a silver tinsel body. This was at Strangford Lough at the end of summer, the time was evening.

Three dozen and nine were brought into the boat, sometimes two at a time and more would have been taken had not a pollack risen to one of the flies, bolted for the weeds, after the manner of these fish, and smashed up the tackle.

John Bickerdyke, Sea Fishing, 1895

A GANG OF THAMES POACHERS
WELL SERVED OUT

O N SATURDAY LAST, 21 September, Solomon Bigley Armitage, John Stokes the younger and Wm Pearce, all of Old Brentford, were summoned before the Richmond Bench of Magistrates by Thos Rosewell, one of the assistant riverkeepers and supported by Mr H. Farnell, the honorary secretary to the Thames Angling Preservation Society.

Mr Farnell shortly stated the case to the bench and said that if he proved the same to the satisfaction of the magistrates, he hoped they would, by their judgement, teach the defendants they would not be permitted to pursue such violent conduct and lawless proceedings, otherwise bloodshed would be the result. He then proceeded with the several cases in the summonses against the defendants, which charged them first, with fishing with a net in the preserve at Twickenham on the night of 10 September; secondly, with using a net between sunset and sunrise at the same time and place, being above Richmond Bridge and thirdly, with having taken certain untakeable fish in their possession, consisting of roach, dace and gudgeon, the above several offences being contrary to the bye laws made pursuant to the statute Geo 30, 2.

The defendants were, in addition, charged with obstructing the riverkeepers in their duty, by refusing to allow them to search the well to examine the fish; and also with striking one of the riverkeepers with a punt pole.

The defendants pleaded guilty to having unsizeable fish in their possession, but not guilty to the other charges. John Rough, Thomas Rosewell and George Howard, all riverkeepers, were then called and their evidence was to the following effect. About two o'clock on Monday morning, 10 September, they were in company with George Francis and Samuel Harris, also riverkeepers, out on duty on the Surrey side of the river, opposite Pope's Villa. Harris was left in charge of the boat. They went on shore and hid up behind the hedge close to the preserve. They saw the defendants in a boat working a dragnet; they then tried to get through the hedge but could not. After watching the defendants for some time they went back to their boat, lying off Petersham Lane. They got into the boat and laid up under Petersham Ait. About five o'clock in the morning the defendants' boat came down with four men in her and a large net on the stern.

The officers then went for the defendants' boat. Rosewell hung on to her with a hitcher when the defendants' watchman, in another boat, ran into the officers' boatside. One of the defendants then, with a pole, made a blow at Rosewell's head, which missed his head but fell on his arm. The pole also fell into the officers' boat. The net was then thrown overboard. Rosewell and Francis then boarded the defendants' boat to search the well. They were obstructed in doing so, the defendants saying it was locked and should not be opened.

The officers then forced it and found between 800 and 900 fish, roach, dace and gudgeon, a large portion being unsizeable fish. They took some away (which were produced in court) after which the boats were separated and went down to Richmond. Rough then saw G. Howard and told him to go and watch the place where the net went overboard until the tide began to flow. He did so and found it and stated it was in every respect an unlawful net.

The net was then produced in court and a more destructive engine was never seen, being about 1in in the mesh throughout, about 100yd in length and heavily loaded with bricks.

The bench consulted for a time and stated they considered all the cases fully proved and fined each of the defendants 5s, including costs and in default of payment to six weeks imprisonment; one week allowed for payment.

Mr Farnell then asked if either of the defendants claimed the net; they replied they knew nothing about it. He then referred to the fifty-fourth item of the bye laws and, referring to the evidence of Howard, called upon the bench to order the same to be forthwith burnt by the police, which was accordingly done.

The Field, 1858